Elite • 161

The US Home Front 1941–45

Alejandro de Quesada • Illustrated by Stephen Walsh

Consultant editor Martin Windrow

First published in Great Britain in 2008 by Osprey Publishing,
Midland House, West Way, Botley, Oxford OX2 0PH, UK
443 Park Avenue South, New York, NY 10016, USA
E-mail: info@ospreypublishing.com

A CIP catalog record for this book is available from the British Library

ISBN: 978 1 84603 208 0

Editor: Martin Windrow
Page layout by Ken Vail Graphic Design, Cambridge, UK
Typeset in Helvetica Neue and ITC New Baskerville
Index by Glyn Sutcliffe
Originated by PPS Grasmere, Leeds, UK
Printed in China through World Print Ltd.

08 09 10 11 12   10 9 8 7 6 5 4 3 2 1

A CIP catalogue record for this book
is available from the British Library

FOR A CATALOGUE OF ALL BOOKS PUBLISHED BY OSPREY MILITARY AND
AVIATION PLEASE CONTACT:

NORTH AMERICA
Osprey Direct, c/o Random House Distribution Center, 400 Hahn Road,
Westminster, MD 21157
E-mail: info@ospreydirect.com

ALL OTHER REGIONS
Osprey Direct UK, P.O. Box 140 Wellingborough, Northants, NN8 2FA, UK
E-mail: info@ospreydirect.co.uk

Osprey Publishing is supporting the Woodland Trust, the UK's leading
woodland conservation charity, by funding the dedication of trees.

Buy online at **www.ospreypublishing.com**

Acknowledgments

I would like to thank the following individuals and
institutions who have contributed to making this book
possible: Jack and Maggie Grothe, Tony Petruso, Marc
Kohlbaum, Alex Solera, Mark Kasal, Martin Windrow, AdeQ
Historical Archives, Jefferson Barracks, The American Red
Cross, The American Field Service, Civil Air Patrol, United
States Coast Guard Auxiliary, National Archives, United
States Public Health Service, Pinellas County Historical
Commission, Walt Disney Productions, United Services
Organizations (USO), National Geodetic Survey, The Boy
Scouts of America, The Girl Scouts of America, National
Association of Civilian Conservation Corps Alumni, and
The Company of Military Historians.

Photographic credits

Unless otherwise indicated, all images are from the
collections of AdeQ Historical Archives Inc.

Artist's note

Readers may care to note that the original paintings from
which the color plates in this book were prepared are
available for private sale. All reproduction copyright
whatsoever is retained by the Publishers. All inquiries
should be addressed to:

info@stevewalsh.co.uk

The Publishers regret that they can enter into no
correspondence upon this matter.

TITLE PAGE **A typical patriotic display in a store window.
The sale of War Bonds provided a crucial source of revenue
for the war effort. Instead of relying upon "passive" selling,
the federal government sponsored public stunts – including
celebrity auctions featuring personalities such as movie
stars and decorated war heroes – to actively sell the war
to the American people.**

THE US HOME FRONT
1941–45

INTRODUCTION

The rapid fall of France to the German Blitzkrieg invasion of May–June 1940 shook but did not destroy the strong isolationist, even pacifist sentiment among the American public. Suddenly, Great Britain stood alone against Nazi Germany, and looked toward the United States for support – which was given, in the form of vitally needed supplies shipped on a "buy now, pay later" basis. As early as 1939 patriotic and service organizations had begun to spring up across the United States in anticipation of the war spreading, and these efforts redoubled as the reports of the Battle of Britain and the bombing of British cities were reported by American radio correspondents into American homes. President Franklin D. Roosevelt was criticized by many as a war-monger for his patient efforts to carry the people with him in turning the United States into the "great arsenal of democracy" during 1940 and 1941; but at the stunning news of the Japanese attack on Pearl Harbor on Sunday, December 7, 1941 patriotic feeling soared in American society, and the United States became fully committed to the war against the dictatorships.

Americans' willingness to carry out blackout and civil defense drills; to save everyday materials for recycling; to work longer hours, while having fewer consumer goods to buy with their salaries – all these demonstrated the nation's strong support for the war. There were more fundamental changes than these habits of thrift: World War II brought about a political, psychological and economic shift to the right in the United States.

The preparations for waging a world war brought new life into depressed and dormant communities across the country. The outbreak of World War II saw enormous numbers of new military airfields and other bases established in many states. The Southeast region became the main focal point for training fighter and bomber aircrews, and the need for more airfields forced the military to convert many sleepy county airports into functioning military facilities.

During wartime, even civilian female fashions reflected patriotic support for the armed forces, as in this advertisement for "sportswear."

For instance, at the beginning of 1940 there were just eight military installations in the state of Florida; by 1943 there were 172.

The federal government encouraged Americans to conserve and recycle all materials that could be used for wartime production. It turned out that lots of everyday household trash had value: kitchen fats, old metal shovels, even empty metal lipstick tubes. The federal government also compelled Americans to cut back on foodstuffs and consumer goods, and ration cards became necessary to purchase such staples as coffee, sugar, and meat. The rationing of gasoline and vehicle tires was particularly shocking in a nation of huge distances and a tradition of freedom to travel. Virtually all kinds of manufactured metal goods became hard to replace. These wartime shortages caused a mounting frustation, since they came at a time of high levels of employment: for the first time in years people had money to spend, but there were few goods available for purchase. When the war finally came to a close in 1945 and industries returned to consumer production, Americans would go on a buying spree of unprecedented proportions.

The necessities of war even influenced American fashion. In the spring of 1942 the War Production Board became the nation's premier clothing consultant by dictating styles for civilian apparel that would conserve cloth for the war effort. For example, menswear rid itself of vests, elbow patches on jackets, and cuffs on pants. Women's clothing was also redesigned to use fewer materials, and skirts became shorter and narrower. *De rigueur* for patriotic women were efficient, two-piece bathing suits, which created the biggest public stir since Mrs Amelia Bloomer; Mr Marcus of the famous Nieman-Marcus department store called these swimsuits "patriotic chic."

The nation at work

The war provided an excuse to abolish segments of the New Deal. Conservative politicians had fought against these agencies for years, but now that President Roosevelt was focusing on winning a war instead of reforming society, they could slash funding for the Civilian Conservation Corps (CCC), Works Projects Administration (WPA), and National Youth Administration (NYA). Congress had always intended these programs to help those Americans who suffered job discrimination, even during favorable economic conditions, so their demise was especially hard on African Americans, women, and the elderly. With the elimination of many New Deal programs, poverty increased for many Americans even at a time of rising wages.

Still, for a great part of the working population the wartime economy brought about full employment and, in doing so, achieved what New Deal programs had been unable to do. In 1940, 8 million Americans were unemployed; during that year, however, this surplus almost disappeared. The high wages offered by many rapidly expanding industries sucked in workers from other parts of the country, particularly from poor rural areas; this, in combination with military enlistments, left these sectors suffering from serious shortages of labor, with dire consequences for many farming families – even though the government was purchasing enormous quantities of some foodstuffs. Another hardship was the chronic lack of housing for the new workers, which meant that many men who found work in war production factories planted in formerly small communities in other states were unable to bring their families with them.

Wives and families

Despite these movements of population, some industries were still short of vital hands, and this led to more and more women taking up factory jobs that had once been reserved for men by the labor unions. "Rosie the Riveter" became a popular American icon, and by 1945 women

June 1942: a housewife gives a pound weight of salvaged, sieved cooking fat back to her butcher for recycling. (Photo Ann Rosener; Library of Congress Prints & Photographs Division)

made up 36 percent of the nation's total workforce. The new freedoms and temptations of wartime led to many family breakdowns, illegitimate births, hasty marriages and divorces. A more positive consequence is less often remembered: when men answered the military draft or traveled to where the work was to be found, many left behind wives who had to fend for themselves. These women often pooled their efforts in raising their families, forming into groups and sharing such chores as cooking, housework, and laundry. Many who had young children shared apartments and houses in order to save time, money, utilities and food. If both worked, they worked different shifts so they could take turns babysitting. For many, this sharing and cooperation born out of the demands placed on the women of World War II created life-long bonds among them.

Life on the home front brought special challenges as those left behind by the disruption of families had to cope with rationing and shortages; many everyday necessities were scarce or simply unobtainable. Families with children were constantly worried about their little ones falling sick; if they were in work, they might be better able than ever before to pay doctor bills, but illnesses that were readily treatable during normal times often became serious because of a general shortage of pharmaceuticals and other medical supplies diverted for military use – particularly antibiotics such as penicillin. But support for the soldiers overseas never lagged. Some people got rich from the wartime boom, but the great majority simply kept working patiently, all of them making their contribution to the eventual victory. In the process, they changed the American workplace forever.

The war threatened the harmony and morale of Americans, and government authorities had to figure out what they could do about it. During the early days of the war baseball hardly seemed a priority, but it was judged to be important for public morale by President Roosevelt. On January 15, 1942 the President issued the "Green Light" letter and informed Baseball Commissioner Kennesaw Mountain Landis that the 1942 major league baseball season should proceed. (However, injuries and military service decimated the rosters of many major league teams.) When the ballplayers went off to fight, many women entered baseball when the All American Girls Professional Baseball League (AAGPBL) was formed. The women kept baseball alive at a time when public interest would otherwise have waned because of the war. Eventually, training camps for the league were established in Havana, Cuba, and Fort Lauderdale, Florida. The AAGPBL ceased to exist after 1954, but in recent years there has been some increase in the public's awareness of women's role in baseball because of the 1992 film *A League of Their Own*. A permanent exhibit highlighting the role of women in baseball now stands in the Baseball Hall of Fame.

The internment of the *Nisei*

The saddest aspect of life in the United States was the internment of Japanese-Americans – a harsh measure which few other Americans challenged in the atmosphere of paranoia immediately following Pearl

A Japanese-American US Navy veteran of World War I defiantly wears his old uniform and American Legion cap as he reports to federal officials for relocation and internment in the aftermath of Pearl Harbor. Many *Nisei* families lost everything during their internment; family businesses collapsed, and they were forced to sell up their properties at short notice for whatever they could get. (National Archives)

Harbor. In February 1942 the US government forced the relocation of all Japanese-Americans from the West Coast, a region that Roosevelt and other political and military leaders considered vulnerable. The government established ten internment camps in Arkansas, Arizona, California, Colorado, Idaho, Utah, and Wyoming, which held a total of 100,000 persons of Japanese ancestry, many of whom were United States citizens. After his reelection in 1944, Roosevelt canceled the evacuation order and the government closed the camps, but much of the human damage was irreversible.

The growth of executive power

During the war there were changes in the composition of the federal bureaucracy. As the federal government continued to cut funding for social programs, many idealists in Roosevelt's "brains trust" became disillusioned and left their posts. Business executives with good managerial skills, but little interest in social reform, quickly filled this political vacuum in FDR's administration: the priorities now had to be production and organization for the war effort. The magazine *Business Week* reported cheerfully: "The war has placed a premium on business talents rather than on 'brain-trusters' and theoreticians. Businessmen are moving up in the New Deal Administration and are replacing the New Dealers as they go." From 1940 to 1945, the number of civilian employees working for the federal government rose from 1 million to nearly 4 million. The war also accelerated the growth of executive power. At war's end, the President and his advisors, more than Congress, seemed to drive the nation's domestic and foreign agenda. Furthermore, the Supreme Court refused to hear cases that challenged this increase in executive authority.

With a minute number of individual exceptions, the only way *Wehrmacht* servicemen got onto US soil was as prisoners of war shipped back to camps in America – like this class photographed during an English lesson at Camp Blanding, Florida. Most POWs were decently treated, though US government inquiries did identify a number of cases of serious abuse. (National Archives)

ENEMY ACTION & HOMEGROWN FASCISM

Because of the United States' geographical isolation, separated by the width of the Atlantic and Pacific Oceans from the battlefronts, some thought that the nation was safe; however, the war did reach its shores.

In January 1942, German submarines arrived off the Atlantic Coast; no serious consideration had been given to the protection of coastal shipping, which included the regular passage of oil tankers from the Gulf coast northwards. By night the U-boat commanders could see their targets outlined against the undimmed lights of the seashore towns, and by May they had already sunk 180 vessels. (They called these months "the second happy time," since it recalled their massacre of British shipping in the western Atlantic following the German capture of the French Atlantic ports in summer 1940.) Some of the U-boat engagements offshore could be seen right from the beaches. Members of the Coast Guard Auxiliary responded to the sinking vessels, rescuing those who were forced to abandon ship, but many seamen drowned or were badly burned. In addition, German submarines (U-202 and U-584) offloaded two teams of saboteurs and explosives on the beaches of Amagansett, Long Island, and Ponte Vedra, Florida.

Even the West Coast had its share of enemy incursions, although the only serious operation was the Japanese invasion of the Aleutian Islands off the coast of Alaska. The carrier air raids and landings on the Aleutians took place in early June 1942, in an attempt to split US Navy forces during the Battle of Midway; the Japanese garrisons presented only a low-priority threat, however, and were allowed to remain until April–May 1943, when Attu was retaken in hard fighting and Kiska was abandoned by the Japanese.

Enemy activity against the mainland was more alarming than dangerous, though it inevitably tied down some US resources in precautionary response. The Imperial Japanese Navy submarine I-17 shelled Ellwood oil refinery at Geleta on the Californian coast on February 23, 1942. A radio station on Estevan Point, Vancouver Island, Canada, was fired on by the Japanese submarine I-26 on June 20, 1942,

US government law enforcement and military personnel examining one of the thousands of Japanese balloon bombs sent drifting across the Pacific. This one – like most of those recovered – came down in open country; the damage they did was negligible. (National Archives)

and the next day the I-25 shelled Fort Stevens, Oregon. In September phosphorus bombs were dropped on Mt Emily, ten miles northeast of Brookings, Oregon, to start forest fires; the aircraft responsible was a Yokosuka E14Yl "Glen" reconnaissance seaplane piloted by Lt Nubuo Fujita, who had been catapulted from the deck of the I-25. Phosphorus bombings were repeated on the southern coast of Oregon a few weeks later.

Balloon bombs

Between November 1944 and April 1945, Japan launched over 9,000 incendiary balloons toward the American mainland. Carried by the Pacific jetstream, these balloons were to sail over the Pacific Ocean and land in North America, where the Japanese hoped they would start forest fires and wreak devastation. About 300 were reported as reaching North America, but little damage was caused. Six people – five children and a woman, Elsie Mitchell – became the only deaths due to enemy action to occur in mainland America during World War II when a balloon exploded while one of the children was trying to recover it from a tree near Bly, Oregon. Another exploded in Omaha, Nebraska, with little effect. Recently released RCMP and Canadian military reports indicate that fire balloons got as far inland as the rural area near Ituna, Saskatchewan. In all the Japanese fire balloons were found in the states of Alaska, Washington, Oregon, California, Arizona, Idaho, Montana, Utah, Wyoming, Colorado, Texas, Kansas, Nebraska, South Dakota, North Dakota, Michigan, and Iowa, as well as in Mexico and Canada. The last known discovery of a viable balloon in North America was in 1955 – its payload still lethal after 10 years of corrosion. A non-lethal balloon bomb was discovered in Alaska as late as 1992.

The German-American *Bund*

Not all enemies were offshore, however; some were homegrown. Various communist, fascist, and other potentially subversive organizations existed in the United States prior to America's entry into the war. These included organizations such as the American National-Socialist Party, Christian Front, The Ultra-American, Nationalist Party, Friends of New Germany, The Gray Shirts, German-American *Bund*, America First Committee, Anglo-Saxon Federation of America, National Workers League, American Patriots, Crusaders for Americanism, Paul Revere Sentinels, and Ku Klux Klan. Known collectively as "fifth columnists" in the jargon of the 1930s (the reference dated from the Spanish Civil War), these organizations sought to undermine US neutrality by giving tacit or overt support to the Axis. Of these, the German-American *Bund* attracted the most attention from the Federal Bureau of Investigation (FBI).

In May 1933 Rudolf Hess, Deputy Führer of the NSDAP (German Nazi party), authorized the formation of an American Nazi party to be known as the "Friends of New Germany;" with assistance from the German consul in New York City, the organization came into existence under the leadership of Heinz Spanknobel. The organization engaged in pro-Nazi activities which included the storming of a German-language newspaper, the *New Yorker Staats-Zeitung*, to demand that more articles sympathetic to the Nazi cause be printed. Eventually Spanknobel was ousted and deported as a "foreign agent." The Friends of New Germany were openly supported by Hitler's government until, in 1935, Nazi officials realized that the organization was doing more harm than good. Hess recalled the leaders to Germany and the group disbanded in December 1935.

In its place, many former members of the "Friends" formed a new organization in March 1936 in Buffalo, New York; this was called the *Amerikadeutscher Volksbund* or German-American League. Fritz Kuhn, a former veteran of the Kaiser's army during World War I, became the organization's *Bundesleiter*; under his leadership the organization became united and its membership grew. A quarter of the League's membership were of German nationality, but the majority were first- and second-generation German immigrants. The German-American *Bund* mimicked the Nazi organization with their version of a uniformed Hitler Youth, to educate its members in German culture – language, history, and literature – as well as indoctrinating them with Nazi ideology. In addition, the League formed an *Ordnungsdienst* (OD) that became its militant arm; OD members wore uniforms based on those of the early Brownshirts (SA). Rallies were soon being held regularly; the *Bund* created recreational camps such as camps Nordland (New Jersey), Siegfried (New York), and Hindenburg (Wisconsin); and German beerhalls in Chicago and Milwaukee were frequent venues for local League meetings. Anti-Semitic attacks by Bundists increased, and the German Foreign Ministry commented that the *Bund* was no different from the earlier Friends of New Germany.

In 1936 a delegation of Bundists led by Kuhn traveled to Berlin for the Summer Olympics, and Kuhn and his followers were invited for a meeting and photo opportunity with Adolf Hitler at the Reichs Chancellery. While it was not the intention of the German Führer, Kuhn exploited every opportunity to use the photographs as evidence of an endorsement of his position as *Bundesführer* of the United States; consequently, the United States authorities began to believe there was

During a meeting of the Congressional Committee on Un-American Activities, Congressman Martin Dies is photographed with a former member of the German-American *Bund* wearing the uniform of the movement's *Frauenschaft*. (See Plate A.)

AMERICA CALLING

Take your place in CIVILIAN DEFENSE

CONSULT YOUR NEAREST DEFENSE COUNCIL

a significant relationship between the Third Reich and the German-American *Bund.*

In 1937 the FBI investigated allegations that 200,000 Bundists were ready to take up arms against the US government. Although they found no evidence for this fantastic claim, in 1938 Martin Dies of the House Un-American Activities Committee investigated the organization. He claimed – wildly – that the *Bund* had 480,000 members; in fact, at its peak in 1938, it had only about 8,500 members and an additional 5,000 or so sympathizers.

The Federal Government's attention on the *Bund* was not considered a problem by German government officials in the United States. The German ambassador, Hans Heinrich Dieckhoff, believed that the League would never succeed because many German-Americans living in the United States were as indifferent to politics as their American counterparts. While the *Bund* was being investigated as a puppet organization serving the ends of Adolf Hitler, in fact the Third Reich gave only the most limited financial or even verbal support to the movement, though there were some unofficial contacts. In order to appease the United States, on March 1, 1938 the German government firmly declared that no German citizen could be a member of the *Bund* and that Nazi emblems were not to be employed by the organization. Kuhn requested a meeting in Berlin with an aide from the Reichs Chancellery and appealed for this decision to be reversed, but was told that the announcement was final.

The German-American League held their largest rally ever in New York's Madison Square Garden in February 1939. A crowd of 22,000 attended, and a detachment of 3,000 OD men provided security for the rally and for Fritz Kuhn. The *Bundesleiter*, under a massive portrait of George Washington and oversized American flags, made a speech attacking the President, calling him "Frank D. Rosenfeld," and accusing the federal government of conspiring with "Bolsheviks." Following the rally Kuhn was arrested by the New York District Attorney for forgery and larceny; this arrest and Kuhn's subsequent imprisonment marked the beginning of the end for the organization. Gerhard Kunze was named the new *Bundesleiter*, but because of political infighting and negative public perception the membership began to decline. The *Bund* was dissolved on December 8, 1941, the day after the attack on Pearl Harbor. Following Germany's declaration of war with the United States, federal officials raided the homes and businesses of *Bund* leaders. Many were arrested for "subversive activities," including Gerhard Kunze, who was apprehended in Mexico and served a 15-year sentence. For conspiring to violate the 1940 Selective Service Act, 24 Bundists were arrested and served time in prison. Some *Bund* leaders committed suicide before federal officials caught up with them; other members had their American citizenship revoked, but the majority were left alone. By June 1942 the last signs of the *Bund* disappeared. After the war Fritz Kuhn was deported by the United States to Germany, where he died as a "persona non grata" in 1951.

HOME DEFENSE & PRE-MILITARY TRAINING

Office of Civilian Defense (OCD)

The OCD was established on May 20, 1941 to coordinate federal, state, and local defense programs for the protection of civilians during air raids and other emergencies, and to facilitate civilian participation in war programs. As an administrative aid, the national OCD organization was divided into nine regional offices, coincident with Army Commands. These offices adopted and explained national programs and offered expert technical advice, but did not actually carry them out – that was left to states and communities.

The local Defense Council was the central planning and coordinating body for all programs relating to community and civilian war effort. As such, it had the responsibility of mobilizing all forces in the community which could help protect the community and prosecute the war. The responsibility extended to the mobilization of civilian volunteers; the Defense Council carried out this charge through the establishment of a Volunteer Office, and the appointment of a Commander of the Citizens Defense Corps and an Executive of the Citizens Service Corps, to which volunteers were referred. With the end of the war the OCD was abolished in June 1945 – only to be revived during the Cold War.

The Civil Defense symbol, consisting of a red "CD" on a white triangle within a blue circle, was created in 1939 by Charles T. Coiner, art director of the N.W. Ayer advertising agency (who also designed the National Recovery Administration's blue eagle). The symbol became familiar to generations of Americans who remembered air raid drills, blackouts, and fallout shelters during the Cold War. Richard Grefe, executive director of the American Institute of Graphic Arts, noted that "the old mark fits in the same category of simplicity and impact occupied by the London Underground map." In 2007 the old symbol of the Office of Civil Defense, now reformed and renamed as the Federal Emergency Agency (FEMA), was retired.

The basic Civil Defense armband insignia was a red "CD" on a white triangle on a blue disc, but other emblems replaced the letters to identify specialist personnel. Some of those illustrated here are (second row) the red airplane of bomb reconnaissance, diagonal stripes of air raid wardens, and shield of auxiliary police; (third row) the flame of fire watchers, the pick of demolition squads, the ladder of rescue workers, and the retort of decontamination squads; (fourth row) medical personnel, their aides, drivers, and messengers, and the cup of emergency feeding stations; (fifth row) the pincers of electrical repairmen, the multiple symbols of instructors, the insignia of chaplains, and the plain "CD" of trainees.

Junior ROTC cadets working out, under the supervision of a cadet officer. They wear Army-style uniforms with distinctive unit shoulder insignia.

Reserve Officers Training Corps & Civilian Military Training Camps

The Reserve Officers Training Corps (ROTC) was formally established by the Defense Act of 1916. For several decades before World War I the Army had provided equipment and annually detailed up to 100 regular officers to support college military training through ROTC programs, but until the defense acts of 1916 and 1920 the program was only loosely associated with the Army's own needs. The new dependence on the National Guard and Organized Reserves for Army expansion, and the establishment of the Officers' Reserve Corps (ORC) as a vehicle to retain college men in the US Army after graduation, gave impetus to a greatly enlarged and better regulated ROTC program after 1920. By 1928 there were ROTC units in 325 schools enrolling 85,000 college and university students. Officers detailed as professors of military science instructed these units, and about 6,000 graduates were commissioned in the ORC each year. Thousands of other college graduates received at least some military training through this inexpensive program, which paid rich dividends in 1940 and 1941 when the nation began mobilizing to meet the threat of war. In addition, a Junior ROTC program was implemented in American high schools in order to prepare youths for college ROTC, military academies, and even for the armed forces.

The Civilian Military Training Camps (CMTC) program was more recent and limited, emerging from the Plattsburg movement just before World War I and the citizens' training camps that it fostered. The Army's CMTC program – a very modest alternative to the system of universal military training proposed in 1919 – provided about 30,000 young

volunteers with four weeks of military training in summer camps each year between 1921 and 1941. Those who completed three, or later four years of CMTC training and related home-study courses became eligible for commissions in the Officers' Reserve Corps. The CMTC thus provided another source of leadership for the Organized Reserves. Although relatively few officers emerged directly from the program, a substantial number of CMTC participants later attended West Point, entered ROTC programs, or received commissions during World War II.

In a motley array of clothing, participants in a Civilian Military Training Camp take a break from an exercise during 1940. The overseas cap is the only common item.

State Defense Forces

Early in the 20th century, Congress elected to have the existing militia known as the "National Guard" placed in a dual capacity. Under the National Defense Act of 1916 a "National Guard of the United States" became an element of the Army for war, but each state retained the training and appointment of officers, and the state National Guard remained available for law enforcement and for emergencies.

During the Mexican Border Service and World War I the National Guard was called into federal service, and for longer than the 90-day limit that has been in effect since 1792. Extended wartime duty left most states without a militia, which in turn led to the creation of State Guards. After the war and throughout the 1920s the National Guards were revived and State Guards disbanded. In 1940 the National Guards were once again called away for training, and their members subsequently served throughout World War II, being effectively merged into the US Army; in consequence of this extended and indefinite absence, the states once more began forming their own defense forces. Every state except for Arizona, Montana, Nevada, and

Non-combatants – such as these Congressmen visiting an American war cemetery overseas and wearing Army-style khakis – might display a large distinctive blue sleeve patch showing the blue letters "US" on a Civil Defense-style triangle (see Plate E2).

Oklahoma eventually had what became known collectively as State Guards.

In addition, the territorial holdings of the United States (Alaska, Hawaii, Samoa, Virgin Islands, and the Commonwealth of Puerto Rico) each had its own equivalent of a defense force. For example, the Hawaii Territorial Guard was formed on December 7, 1941 – the day of the Japanese attack – and was initially composed of a large percentage of ROTC cadets of the University of Hawaii. The old Provisional Police of Hilo made up some of the approximately 4,500 members of the Hawaii Rifles, a unit of the Territorial Guard. Many members of the new Hawaiian Territorial Guard wore improvised white armbands with black block letters "HTG" before distinctive shoulder patches for the various units were adopted a few months later.

Perhaps the most interesting of these territorial defense force units were the ones raised in American Samoa. In 1904 the naval governor of Samoa had formed the Fita Fita Guard and Band, and the native recruits were to serve as landsmen for the naval station located on the island. In addition, the Fita Fita were trained as combatants, medical personnel, code personnel, and for such duties as ship repairs. Prior to the spread of World War II to the Pacific, the governor of American Samoa forwarded a letter, dated February 13, 1941, to the Chief of Naval Operations, about the establishment of a native insular force. The first recruits enlisted on August 16, 1941 into the First Samoan Battalion, US Marine Corps Reserve, and came under the control of the local Marine Corps commander; thereafter the unit took on a more marine appearance than their naval Fita Fita counterparts. The unit was conceived as a means of defending the possessions of American Samoa, and was not intended for service in other theaters of the war.

The Samoan Marine unit disbanded on January 15, 1944 with nine Marine officers, one Navy officer, 32 American and 494 Samoan Marines on its rolls. The former First Samoan Battalion's personnel were assigned to the Marine Barracks at the US Naval Station Tutuila for the duration of the war. These units were the only territorial defense forces to be under the control of the Navy and Marine Corps rather than that of the Army and its National Guard components. Both the Fitas and the Samoan Marines were of inestimable value during the months immediately following Pearl Harbor. When the Navy left American Samoa after World War II, most of the Fita Fita transferred to Hawaii (the first significant out-migration of American Samoans to the US). The uniforms of the two organizations were similar in style except for the headgear; the Fitas wore a stiff red cloth band about 3in wide around the head, leaving the hair on the scalp exposed; for general duties a white *lava-lava* was worn (the Samoan word for the skirt, as well as for clothing in general), and one of dark blue color for dress. They wore a red sash around the waist with both the white and blue *lava-lava*s. The men of the First Samoan Battalion, USMC Reserve wore white tee-shirts with red-trimmed khaki overseas caps and *lava-lava*s; an improvised USMC emblem was worn on both items.

* * *

During the war several states had paramilitary organizations which acted as "umbrella" units, serving within the state and performing "guard-like" functions, which in most cases were independent of that state's Defense forces. These carried out rear-echelon duties such as first aid, transportation, and communications. Organizations such as the American Women's Voluntary Services, Women's Ambulance and Defense Corps of America, Massachussetts Home Defense Corps, and the Watchman/Federal Guard unit of Puerto Rico are examples of some of these groups that served alongside many state guard units during World War II.

With very few qualified military personnel available for instruction, the special training of the Boy Scouts of America (BSA) was recognized by the commanders of the State Guards of America, who made the greatest use of it and appointed Scout instructors to their Tactical School. The results of the training the Scouters gave to embryo State

Members of the Fita Fita Guard in American Samoa; while they, and the 1st Samoan Marine Bn, came under US Navy command, they were in fact a territorial defense force. The blue stripes on the *lava-lava* identify ratings: two for apprentice seaman, three for seaman second class, and four for seaman first class. The higher ratings were identified by regular US Navy badges placed above the stripes, as just visible on the foreground man in the front rank.

Men of the Florida Defense Force (later, Florida State Guard) undergo marksmanship training; note the wide variety of clothing and headgear. Some are wearing the distinctive alligator patch – see Plate F – on their caps. (Pinellas County Historical Commission)

Guardsmen were extremely encouraging. The Scouters imparted their instruction by means of a "learning by doing" process, treating the recruits much as they treated Cubs and Scouts. "Do not be surprised," said MajGen Sherman Miles, commanding the 1st Corps Area of the United States Army, when opening the Tactical School, "if we frankly teach you Boy Scout Law. We grown men and soldiers may have thought we were beyond such elementary games. We were mistaken." The "games" to which the general referred were adaptations of the old Kim game – stalking, hiding, and personal camouflage. There was also an obstacle hike during which trainees met with such barriers to forward progress as "bottomless canyons" and electric fences. The course ended with instruction in tracking, based on Baden-Powell's original work on that subject.

Some states had State Guard organizations that remained intact over many years. The New York Guard was formed in 1914 and has been active ever since – it never closed between the World Wars – and various other State Guard programs survived the peacetime years. In 1947 most of the State Guards were closed down and all National Guards were reorganized.

PATRIOTIC SERVICE ORGANIZATIONS

United Service Organizations

The mission of the USO was stated to be to enhance the quality of life of the personnel within US Armed Forces military communities, and to create partnership between US military and civilian communities worldwide.

In 1941 President Roosevelt requested that six organizations provide on-leave recreation for members of the US Armed Forces, the great majority of whom would find themselves spending their brief off-duty time in strange cities far from home. The Salvation Army, YMCA, YWCA, National Catholic Community Services, National Jewish Welfare Board, and National Travelers' Aid Association coordinated to form the USO (United Service Organizations). Despite the conflicts and uncertainty of the decades that followed, USO has endured, and continues to provide "a touch of home" for US forces to this day. The USO is a private, non-profit, civilian organization, which works in cooperation with the military to provide service to military personnel and their families. During the war the USO filled a critical role in community participation in the war effort. USO facilities were found everywhere: in churches, log cabins, museums, barns, and even railroad cars. At its high point in 1944 the USO had over 3,000 clubs. The USO was many things to many people: a lively place to dance and meet people, see movies, have free coffee and donuts, write letters or just relax. The USO all but disbanded in 1947, and then resurfaced during the Korean War when the Department of Defense required expansion of troops around the globe – so the USO expanded with them.

Early in the war the only uniformed representatives of the USO were the Salvation Army. Salvation Army Representatives always worked in a trim gray uniform of lightweight serge with matching hat; the collar bore a strip of blue felt, resembling a British officer's gorget patch, bearing a silver "S" and the rank insignia of the wearer. Women wore a gray silk blouse, navy-blue tie, off-black or gunmetal hose and black shoes. The overseas cap had a red cord piping and a rank insignia pinned to the wearer's left side. Eventually USO members and entertainers serving in camp shows overseas wore US Army-style uniforms with "USO" pins on their lapels. In keeping with the USO desire to give a "home away from home" to the service man, USO hostesses did not ordinarily wear uniforms, and were identified only by an armband.

Daughters of the Defenders of the Republic

The Daughters of the Defenders of the Republic was a national patriotic organization, founded by

Many entertainers, such as Marlene Dietrich, joined the United Services Organization to provide morale-boosting shows for US servicemen at home and abroad. Photographed here wearing an Army-style uniform with USO insignia, the sultry-voiced Dietrich was particularly known for singing the English language version of *Lili Marlene*, the German forces' favorite enthusiastically adopted by Allied personnel in North Africa.

Mrs Amanda Shaw Hirsch in 1918. Members were descendants of men who served the United States in previous wars, or relatives of loved ones currently serving in the armed forces. The Defenders Corps was started in 1940 in anticipation of the next World War. The corps established recreational canteens for servicemen, with a special emphasis on the Merchant Marine. The organization also got involved with salvage drives, first aid classes, and preparatory training of volunteer workers for hospital and other emergency duties. For discipline and precision, military drills were held weekly under the supervision of Army officers. Associate members of the Defenders Corps did not need to be American citizens, but had to pledge allegiance to the American flag.

American Women's Voluntary Services

The AWVS was a national organization created in anticipation of war, the first office being opened by Mrs Alice T. McLean in January 1940 in Cooperstown, New York. The organization was open to women, irrespective of race, creed or color, who were loyal to the principles of the government of the United States, and was strictly non partisan and non political. Their purpose was to mobilize and train women and place them where they could render the greatest service to the community, state, and nation in time of peace as well as war. The aim was to cooperate with established agencies, maintaining an AWVS program so flexible and varied that it could readily be adapted to meet any emergency needs. The organization had the following services and activities: Motor Transport Service, Volunteer Placement, Volunteer Workshop, Canteen Corps, War Savings Stamps and Bonds, Salvage,

The comedy film star Mickey Rooney hamming it up for the troops; oddly, he seems to wear a hunting knife on his belt.

Victory Pastime, Child Care, Harvesting, Junior Auxiliary, Mending and Repair Service, Fingerprinting, Legal Advice Bureaus, Emergency Switchboard Service, Bureau of Arts and Decorations, War Service Photography, Radio, Recreational, Recruiting, and Typing and Clerical Service. The AWVS boasted a membership of 350,000, under the motto "Unite and Serve."

The AWVS uniform was blue-gray, made of either wool or lightweight cotton and rayon material. The tunic was of military cut, fastened with four large simulated brass front buttons; epaulets of self material were fastened on each shoulder with small buttons; there were four pockets with small buttons on the flaps, and two small buttons on each sleeve. The AWVS emblem was worn on the upper left sleeve. The skirt was straight cut with a single inverted pleat in front; regulation shoes were four-eyelet brown oxfords with sensible heels, worn with tan stockings. The white or light blue shirt, masculine in style, was worn with a navy-blue tie. Brown leather belts and either white or brown leather gloves were worn.

Either an overseas cap or a visored "legionnaire" cap might be worn with the uniform. The latter was reinforced, with a flat top and a squared 2in visor, and was to be worn straight across the eyebrows, with the AWVS membership pin in the center of the band just above the visor. The AWVS pin was also worn on the left side of the overseas cap, 1½in off center. The Motor Transport Service wore a special cap with a

Not all entertainers were flesh-and-blood; Disney were just one of several studios producing animated features with cartoon characters fighting the Axis or living life on the home front. Here Donald Duck is seen in the 1942 cartoon *Der Fuehrer's Face*, taking his last carefully hoarded coffee-bean from a safe. This is a period press release photo, marking the film's achievement of an Academy Award the following year. (Courtesy Walt Disney Productions) soft visor and a round MTS insignia worn on the front; they also had a special top coat.

The uniform of the Junior Auxiliary of the AWVS was a shirtwaist-type dress of bright light blue, of a rayon-wool blend material. It had two breast pockets and epaulets with small AWVS buttons, and closed down the front to the waist with the same buttons. A brown leather belt was worn; the Junior cap was of the overseas style, in the same material as the dress, and bore the Junior pin. Juniors might wear white ankle socks and had to wear sensible, low-heeled shoes.

Bundles for America

Bundles for America was a direct outgrowth of Bundles for Britain. When Lend-Lease brought British ships into American harbors, the women began to work directly with the crews, and these contacts revealed to them that sailors too – of both nationalities – needed their generosity; thus Bundles for Bluejackets was born. After Pearl Harbor, requests came in to Bundles for Bluejackets to perform the same service for the Army as well, and the more inclusive name Bundles for America was adopted. Almost simultaneously, the President's War Relief Board asked that no agency carry out both foreign and domestic relief;

Sex appeal enlisted in the patriotic cause, at the same time as advertising Chesterfield cigarettes; Deanne Furneau is depicted here in the uniform of the Motor Transport Corps of the American Women's Voluntary Services.

Bundles for America therefore incorporated as a separate entity, working only with American armed forces.

Bundles for America was a national non-profit war relief organization which knitted regulation garments to fill official requests from the Army, Navy, Coast Guard and Merchant Marine, and provided clothing for the families of men whose lives had been disrupted by war. With the exception of necessary office assistance, all executives, knitters and sewers were volunteers, and those who knitted made the contribution not only of their labor, but of the cost of the yarn. Upon request it furnished the government's day rooms at Army posts and air bases. It supplied libraries and comforts for soldiers and sailors in hospitals; equipped music rooms in large encampments, and hospital porches; and mended and repaired clothing at large posts. Thousands of "service kits" were distributed, containing many necessary items specifically desired by men at points of debarkation and to survivors of sea battles and disasters. After the Japanese attack on Pearl Harbor the organization adopted the slogan "Let's Hit Back Hard," and this was found on the organization's sleeve emblem, a gold eagle on a blue shield.

The official uniform of the organization was made of dark blue material composed entirely of aralac and rayon, processed to reduce wrinkling to the minimum. The semi-fitted unbelted jacket fastened with self-color plastic buttons, and had shoulder epaulets and four button-flap pockets. The shoulder patch was worn on the upper left sleeve and a similiar emblem on the front of a visored hat made of the uniform material. The skirt was straight and slim, with kick pleats at front and back. A classic white shirt was worn with its notched collar opening over the suit collar and lapels. A shoulder-strap bag of matching gabardine trimmed with blue leather, low-heeled shoes and white gloves completed the uniform.

National Security Women's Corps

The NSWC was founded in June 1940, and a year later was incorporated by approximately 200 women who wanted to serve their country in some capacity; this semi-military organization required members to have standard first aid and regular military drill skills. The Corps was composed chiefly of businesswomen, who gave weekends and evenings to volunteer work; they formed "readiness groups," each of which required certain courses which were constantly reviewed to keep members ready for any emergency. There were units in New York, New Jersey, Florida, and Washington, DC. Of the 200,000 hours given to volunteer work, more than half were devoted to supplying the Armed Forces with clerical help at the various recruiting stations. After new members were screened for proof of American citizenship, high school or college graduation, and a doctor's certificate of health, a series of courses were open for them to begin their NSWC training in the following fields: Military Drill and Courtesies (compulsory), Standard First Aid (compulsory), Advanced First Aid, Home Nursing, Nutrition, Air Raid Precaution, Riflery, Communications, Map Reading, Motor Mechanics, Canteen, Photography, Switchboard, Physical Fitness, and Public Speaking.

The uniform, consisting of a gray-blue suit, was identical to that worn by the Office of Civil Defense, but with a woven red shield insignia on the left sleeve. The regulation white shirt was finished with a navy-blue tie. The privates and non commissioned officers wore an overseas cap and the commissioned officers a visored hat. The NSWC pin was worn on the left side of the overseas cap and centered on the front of the visored hat.

National Women's Council of the Navy League

The National Women's Council of the Navy League of the United States was organized in January 1942 by Mrs Robert Weeks Kelley, for the purpose of rendering all possible aid and assistance – supplementing that extended by the US government – to officers and men of the US Navy and the Merchant Marine. It was a branch from the Navy League of the United States, organized in 1902 in

A member of the American Red Cross (right) giving assistance to an Army NCO; only the ARC insignia on the former's uniform distinguish it from that of an Army officer.

the interests and furtherance of "naval preparedness." The women's branch shared in the program and activities of the League, and in addition sought to bolster morale by helping to solve family problems that might arise during a serviceman's enforced absence. Their slogan at the time was "If You Can't Join the Navy ... Join the Navy League."

The uniform of the NWC consisted of a navy-blue suit with epaulets, brass buttons, and navy-blue leather belt, with the Navy League's anchor insignia on the left sleeve; it was worn with a plain white shirt and navy-blue four-in-hand tie. The overseas cap, worn only by members of the Canteen and Motor Corps, carried the insignia on the left side, while the visored hat worn by all other members of the League bore the insignia in front. The navy-blue overcoat was single-breasted, with navy-blue belt, brass buttons, and the insignia again on the left arm. The insignia also decorated the navy-blue uniform dress, which had a white gilet in addition to brass buttons, blue leather belt, and epaulets.

HUMANITARIAN ORGANIZATIONS

A senior female member of the American Red Cross wearing its blue-gray uniform – see Plate D1. Note the pin with five stars; this indicates that she has five family members serving in the US armed forces.

The American Red Cross

During World War II the ARC was called upon to provide extensive services to the US military, the Allies, and civilian war victims. It enrolled more than 104,000 nurses for military service; prepared 27 million packages for American and Allied prisoners of war; and shipped more than 300,000 tons of supplies overseas. At the military's request, the Red Cross also initiated a national blood donor program that collected 13.3 million pints for use by the armed forces.

American Red Cross involvement in World War II preceded the entrance of the United States into the conflict. When hostilities began in Europe in 1939 the Red Cross became the chief provider of relief supplies for the civilian victims of conflict, distributed by the Geneva-based International Red Cross Committee. In February 1941 the Red Cross responded to a request by the US government to begin a Blood Donor Service to produce lifesaving plasma for the armed forces in anticipation of America's entry into the war. After the attack on Pearl Harbor the Red Cross quickly mobilized a volunteer and staff force to fulfill the mandates of its 1905 congressional charter, which required that the organization "furnish volunteer aid to the sick and wounded of armies in time of war," and "act in matters of voluntary relief and in accord with the military and naval authorities as a medium of

communication between the people of the United States of America and their Army and Navy."

At home, millions of volunteers provided comfort and aid to members of the armed forces and their families; they served in hospitals suffering from severe shortages of medical staff, produced emergency supplies for war victims, collected scrap, ran "victory gardens," and maintained training programs in home nutrition, first aid and water safety. Overseas, Red Cross workers served as field directors, providing compassionate support for the troops they accompanied; they operated clubs and mobile canteens for the armed forces, and were attached to military hospitals, hospital ships, and hospital trains. At the peak of Red Cross wartime activity in 1945, 7.5 million volunteers were on the rolls, along with 39,000 paid staff. Throughout the war years, the Red Cross served a total of 16 million military personnel, including one million combat casualties. By the time the war ended in September 1945 the American public had contributed over $784 million in support of the American Red Cross. Nearly every family in America contained a member who had either served as a Red Cross volunteer, made contributions of money or blood, or was a recipient of Red Cross services.

General Dwight D. Eisenhower, in an address to Congress on June 18, 1945, acknowledged that "The Red Cross, with its clubs for recreation, its coffee and donuts in the forward areas, its readiness to meet the needs of the well and to help minister to the wounded . . . has often seemed to be the friendly hand of this nation, reaching across the sea to sustain its fighting men."

The Public Health Service

The origins of the PHS may be traced to the passage of an act in 1798 that provided for the care and relief of sick and injured merchant seamen. A reorganization in 1870 converted the loose network of locally controlled hospitals into a centrally controlled Marine Hospital Service, with its headquarters in Washington, DC. The position of Supervising Surgeon (later Surgeon General) was created to administer the service, and John Maynard Woodworth was appointed as the first incumbent in 1871. He moved quickly to reform the system, and adopted a military model for his medical staff, instituting examinations for applicants and putting his physicians in uniform. Woodworth created a cadre of mobile, career service physicians who could be assigned as needed to the various marine hospitals. The uniformed services component of the Marine Hospital Service was formalized as the Commissioned Corps by legislation enacted in 1889. At first open only to physicians, over the course of the 20th century the Corps expanded to include dentists, sanitary engineers, pharmacists, nurses, sanitarians, scientists and other health professionals.

As immigration increased dramatically in the late 19th century, the federal government also took over from the individual states the processing of immigrants, beginning in 1891. The Marine Hospital Service was assigned responsibility for the medical inspection of arriving immigrants at sites such as Ellis Island in New York. Commissioned officers played a major role in fulfilling the Service's commitment to prevent disease from entering the country. The PHS performed active wartime service during 1898 by supporting military forces during the Spanish-American War. Both Army and Navy personnel were treated in the PHS marine hospitals, and yellow fever was confronted by PHS officers sent on emergency duty to front-line positions in Cuba and Puerto Rico. The PHS Commissioned Corps accompanied troop transports, staffed temporary quarantine stations, and saw combat within the fleet at the battle of Manila Bay in the Philippines. Because of its broadening responsibilities the name of the service was changed in 1902 to the Public Health and Marine Hospital Service, and again in 1912 to simply the Public Health Service. The PHS continued to expand its public health activities in the 20th century, with the Commissioned Corps leading the way; they helped control the spread of contagious diseases such as smallpox and yellow fever, conducted important biomedical research, regulated the food and drug supply, provided health care to under-served groups, supplied medical assistance in the aftermath of disasters, and served in numerous other ways.

President Wilson invoked the Act of July 1, 1902 to militarize the PHS by executive order on April 3, 1917. Although confirmed by a Congressional resolution of July 9, 1917, this militarization was later repealed by the US Attorney General on October 29, 1921. He ruled

A member of the Cadet Nurse Corps (right) is presented to Mrs Churchill, wife of the British prime minister. Note the silver Public Health Service insignia on the nurse's beret, the Maltese cross shoulder patch, and the transverse shoulder straps ending in buttons (see Plate D3).

that only Congress could create a military force from a civilian agency; the PHS could be utilized alongside the armed forces, but could not be transformed into part of them.

President Roosevelt put the PHS under his newly created Federal Security Agency with effect from July 1, 1939. The FSA was established to promote social and economic security, educational opportunity, and the health of American citizens. When America mobilized during 1940 the PHS prepared for war. In November 1941 the Coast Guard was militarized, and PHS officers served as its medical branch; nearly 700 of them saw combat duty with the USCG during World War II, including nurses from 1944.

When the US declared war in December 1941 many PHS officers were immediately detailed to the Army and Navy. All PHS programs experienced tremendous growth, and the number of personnel increased from 8,000 in 1940 to over 16,000 by 1945. The Commissioned Corps of the PHS employed top-rate doctors, highly trained scientific personnel and nurses of the finest quality. The Service was consolidated during 1943 to comprise four main components: the Office of the Surgeon General, the National Institute of Health, and the new Bureau of Medical Services and Bureau of State Services. The 1944 Public Health Service Act further strengthened the medical and administrative authority of the service and its Surgeon General.

The PHS was active in most health areas during the war, ensuring adequate public health services, strengthening medical assistance to the states, and working in disease prevention; malaria control around military camps and training sites was supervised by the Malaria Control in War Areas program. Late in the war the PHS established an Office of International Health Relations to handle increasing overseas health concerns. Medical services were provided to the United Nations Relief and Rehabilitation Administration within refugee camps in Europe and the Near East.

The service also supported research into many aspects of health care on the home front. For instance, it investigated hazardous substances to protect war factory workers; it examined new explosives, developed methods to determine the amount of lead or TNT in urine (so that workers could be tested for overexposure), and demonstrated the affinity of lead for bone tissue. Other investigators determined that the vapors of methyl, ethyl, isopropyl, and butyl alcohol were acutely toxic to workers. This work improved conditions of employment for more than 300,000 workers in wartime industries.

Treatment of tropical diseases was undertaken at the PHS Rocky Mountain Laboratory in Hamilton, Montana, where yellow fever and typhus vaccines were prepared for military forces. In Bethesda,

Maryland, a synthetic substitute for quinine was sought to treat malaria. Sampling techniques were developed to avoid bacterial contamination in plasma and blood. The PHS revealed that sodium deficiency was a direct cause of death after burns or traumatic shock, leading to the widespread use of oral saline therapy as a first-aid measure on the battlefield. PHS military physiologists researched problems of high-altitude flying; they determined the altitude at which oxygen needed to be given, and designed an apparatus to supply the extra oxygen efficiently. They also studied the relation of pressure changes to bubble formation in liquids to address the problem of embolisms forming in the blood of pilots. Other tests were made to evaluate the efficiency of flight clothing, especially electrically heated suits; to determine the effect of altitude on visual ability; and with devices to improve night vision.

The severe wartime shortage of nurses resulted in a uniformed **Cadet Nurse Corps** as part of the PHS under the Nurse Training Act of 1943. Participants received scholarships and monthly payments to attend nursing schools by agreeing to work in essential nurse positions after graduation for the duration of the war. The program graduated 124,000 nurses, of whom over 3,000 were from the African American and other minorities.

Since the PHS Commissioned Corps was one of the US uniformed services, officers were authorized by the agency to which they were assigned to wear various uniforms. These were mostly purchased from US Navy sources, and officers were required to own a service dress blue uniform. The legal entanglement over USPHS military status was avoided during World War II, because President Roosevelt was given direct Congressional authority to militarize the service, effective from November 11, 1943; but although the Public Health Service Act of July 1, 1944 reinforced the militarization, a few anomalies remained. The Commissioned Corps was expanded in 1944 to include female scientific personnel and nurses, and there was a practical need to designate the PHS as a military force in all regards. For example, some nurses were detailed to secret organizations like the Office of Strategic Services (OSS); this required confirmation of full PHS military capacity to serve in combat, regardless of mission scope or secrecy. Therefore, on June 21, 1945 President Truman signed Executive Order No.9575 that declared "the Commissioned Corps of the Public Health Service to be a military service and a branch of the land and naval forces of the United States during the period of the present war."

American Women's Hospitals Reserve Corps

The AWHRC was a uniformed organization of volunteers trained to serve the community in time of war and peace. It was conceived by Dr Luvia Willard of Jamaica, New York, Secretary of the Board of the American Women's Hospitals, which was formed in 1917 as a War Service Committee of the American Medical Women's Association. Early in 1940 Dr Willard suggested that a group of "lay" women be trained to augment the services of the medical agencies in time of disaster. She was given authority to form such an organization, and was appointed National Director of the AWHRC, with Mrs John Adikes as Co-Director. During World War II the AWHRC became a well trained organization of more than 10,000 members, with units in many states (as well as one in Argentina). The Corps was organized along semi-military lines and was divided into the following divisions of service: Medical, Transportation, Administration, and Supplementary. It was a uniformed corps, though the uniform was not compulsory, and rank was awarded on the basis of achievement. The units met once a week in an armory for two-hour military drills given by members of the military police, state guardsmen or veterans' organizations; during these sessions instruction was given in teamwork, discipline, coordination and physical fitness. Members also served in the selling of War Bonds and Stamps, in the Speaker's bureau, and as hospital workers.

Women's Ambulance and Defense Corps of America
The WADCA came into existence in Los Angeles, California, in November 1940. Female members were trained in infantry drill as well as both standard and advanced first aid. In addition members could take optional courses in ambulance and heavy vehicle driving, rescue squad work, litter drill, chemical warfare, nutrition, home nursing and military first aid. The organization participated in American Red Cross first aid classes, sold War Bonds, handled sandbags and cement, worked in canteens, served as ambulance drivers and chauffeurs, and visited veterans' hospital wards. Interestingly, there was even a cavalry unit within the organization: a photo exists of a mounted WADCA color guard with the United States Flag and a uniquely designed WADCA cavalry "regimental" standard, and one of the members is seen saluting with a US cavalry saber. The circular emblem of the WADCA bore a red eagle with a shielded "A" over a blue cross with the letters "W," "A," "D," and "C." While most of the members were in California, there were representatives in states such as Nevada and New York. The group even had a Disney-designed mascot, consisting of a female centaur in WADCA uniform holding a first aid kit.

Junior American Nurse Inc
The Junior American Nurse Inc was founded in 1939 by Mrs Dixie Love Dean, to train young girls of high school age with a special emphasis in the fields of nursing, nutrition and child care. JAN activities included voluntary work as nurse's aides and helpers in nursery schools, play schools and canteens. Courses included first aid, home nursing, child care, nutrition, and playground leadership. It was thus not only a wartime agency, but also proposed to prepare its young members for life and help them to select their vocation.

The uniform worn by the JAN consisted of a jacket, skirt and top coat in soldier-blue wool. The fitted suit was fastened with three brass buttons bearing an etched gold cross. A white cotton shirt was worn with a bright red four-in-hand necktie. The soldier-blue top coat was double breasted, with deep lapels, four brass buttons, and a half-belt in back. A maritime-style narrow red line on wide navy-blue stripes on the sleeve denoted rank. The hat was an off-the-face model in the same material as the suit, generally resembling a nurse's cap, with a frontal insignia and a red ribbon across the back. Girls in training wore a fitted jumper dress of the same blue, with white blouse and red tie; when courses were completed the trainee could wear the jacket.

American Field Service

The AFS was born as an auxiliary military hospital in Paris during World War I. The volunteer-run, civilian-financed and unarmed American Ambulance, an extension of the nearby American Hospital of Paris, opened its doors in September 1914, and by the end of the Great War 2,500 men had served with the AFS. During World War II, a total of 2,196 AFS volunteers served with the armies of many nations, alongside British, Free French, Canadian, Indian, and South African troops. Their ambulances carried more than a million casualties; 36 AFS drivers were killed, 68 wounded and 13 taken prisoner. The AFS wore a variety of uniforms but the most common types were those used by the British Army, including but not limited to the wool Battledress uniform while serving in Europe, and the Khaki Drill cotton shirts, slacks and shorts while in North Africa or Italy during hot weather.

These members of the Water Division of the Army Transportation Service are civilians, though they wear uniforms similar to those of the other American maritime services. The captain, wearing the blue "reefer" jacket, is identified by his four sleeve rings below a fouled anchor; the petty officer in khakis displays a helmsman's wheel device on his cap.

MARITIME SERVICES

The Army Transport Service

The ATS was organized in late 1898 as an integral part of the Army Quartermaster Department. The concept of an Army-operated fleet had its origins in the experiences of the military sealift during the Spanish-

A US Maritime Service petty officer, with the rating of chief boatswain's mate, teaches an apprentice how to tie an eye-splice. The old salt's insignia are based on those of the US Coast Guard, who supervised Merchant Marine training up to the early months of World War II, when the War Shipping Administration took over.

American War, when US-flagged commercial shipping was found to be inadequately responsive to the Army's needs. During the early 20th century the Army operated a large trans-Pacific sealift, consisting of its own ships as well as a number of commercial vessels, partly of foreign registry. These were time-chartered to support American troops during the Philippine Insurrection and the Relief of Peking. Following 1904, a somewhat skeletonized fleet remained in service until the entry of the United States into World War I, when it was rapidly expanded. By early 1918 Army crews were manning in excess of 50 ships in support of the American Expeditionary Force in France. In July 1918, beset by disciplinary problems with its employees, the War Department requested that the Navy's Overseas Transportation Service take over the Army-operated fleet, but this had not been completely accomplished by the time of the Armistice. Starting in early 1919, the Army began taking back its historic sealift function. With the severe reduction in military requirements which took place beginning in 1921, the fleet reverted to a small nucleus of mainly transports engaged in serving American holdings in the Pacific.

(continued on page 41)

GERMAN-AMERICAN *BUND*, 1939–42
1: Fritz Kuhn, *Bundesführer*
2: Drum Major, *Jugendschaft, Ortsgruppe Brooklyn*
3: Youth Leader, *Frauenschaft*

A

CIVIL DEFENSE
1: US Citizen's Service Corps
2: Black-Out Warden
3: Spotter, Aircraft Warning Service
4: Educational advisor, Civilian Conservation Corps

B

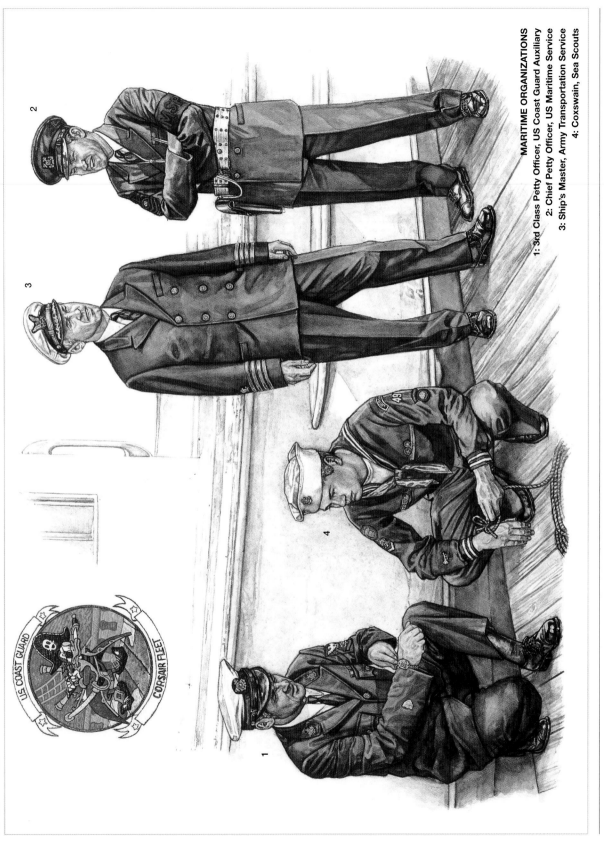

MARITIME ORGANIZATIONS
1: 3rd Class Petty Officer, US Coast Guard Auxiliary
2: Chief Petty Officer, US Maritime Service
3: Ship's Master, Army Transportation Service
4: Coxswain, Sea Scouts

C

HUMANITARIAN ORGANIZATIONS
1: Clubmobile Volunteer, American Red Cross
2: 1st Lt, American Women's Hospital Reserve Corps
3: Cadet Nurse, US Public Health Service
4: Senior Surgeon, US Public Health Service

D

AERONAUTICAL ORGANIZATIONS

1: Flight instructor, BFTS No.5

2: 1st Officer, Air Transport Command

3: Major, 3rd Coastal Patrol, Civil Air Patrol

4: Pilot, Women's Airforce Service Pilots

E

STATE DEFENSE FORCES
1: Sergeant, Florida Defense Force
2: Captain, 4th Regt, Missouri State Guard
3: Private, Women's Ambulance & Defense Corps of America

F

PATRIOTIC ORGANIZATIONS
1: 2nd Lt, Motor Transport, American Women's Volunteer Services
2: National Commander, Daughters of the Defenders of the Republic
3: Entertainer, United Services Organization
4: Volunteer, Junior Commandos

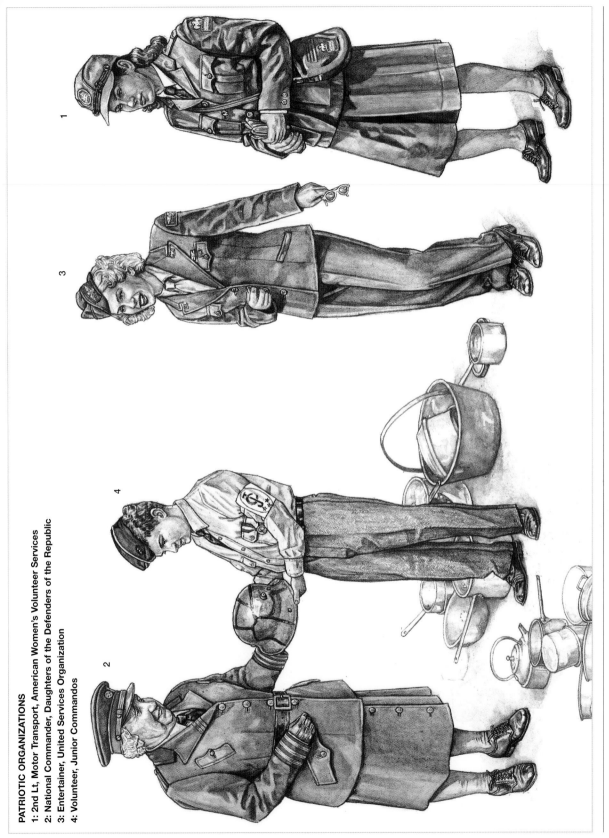

THE WORK FORCE
1: Woman Ordnance Worker, Springfield Armory
2: Auxiliary Military Policeman, St Louis Ordnance Plant
3: Volunteer, Women's Land Army

H

With the beginning of World War II the fleet was again expanded. In 1942 the ATS was absorbed into the Army's Transportation Corps, becoming part of the Water Division, its civilian seamen employees being classified as members of the Water Division's "Civilian Branch." At peak strength during the war the Army's owned and bareboat chartered fleet have been enumerated as follows:

Self-propelled vessels over 1,000 gross tons and over 200 feet LOA: 35 large troop transports; 16 cargo; 55 inter-island; 2 cable-laying; 1 news and communication; 36 floating, self-propelled warehouse, repair, spare parts, and miscellaneous; and 23 hospital ships. With but few exceptions, the large-tonnage ships were manned by civilian seamen of the Water Division; of the large-tonnage fleet, 31 vessels were lost to either enemy action or marine casualty.

Self-propelled vessels less than 1,000 gross tons and less than 200 feet LOA but over 65 feet: 510 freight supply; 104 Y-class tankers; 746 tugs of various classes. The small craft were in part manned by the Civilian Branch of the Water Division and in part by military crews from the Army and/or Coast Guard, the latter operating under Army control. Of the small-tonnage fleet, 28 vessels were lost either to enemy action or marine casualty.

During the war the Army's civilian seamen labor force numbered at peak strength approximately 15,000 men. Throughout the war, it has been estimated that a total of around 20,000 civilians were employed by the Army aboard those vessels which saw service outside of the US continental limits. The Transportation Corps, Water Division (Civilian Branch) suffered a total of 529 men lost to enemy action or marine casualty. The Navy's Military Sea Transport Service took over the Army's prior role in oceangoing shipping during the early 1950s. The Army Transportation Corps still operates a substantial fleet of small craft, the crews of which are now all military.

Excellent study of the uniforms worn by seamen, petty officers (left) and officers (right) of the US Maritime Service in the latter part of the war.

Members of a St Louis flotilla of the US Coast Guard Auxiliary, serving as Temporary Reservists. Note the officer-style tunics being worn with enlisted rating insignia. Such "TRs" were often employed for patrolling local waters, guarding government facilities, and other rear-echelon support duties.

Coast and Geodetic Survey

The National Geodetic Survey, the nation's first civilian scientific agency, was established by President Thomas Jefferson in 1807 as the Survey of the Coast. Its mission soon included surveys of the interior as the nation grew westward. In 1878 the agency was reorganized and renamed the Coast and Geodetic Survey (C&GS); this existed until 1970, when a reorganization created the National Oceanic and Atmospheric Administration (NOAA), with the National Ocean Service (NOS) as a line office.

The Coast & Geodetic Survey and the Weather Bureau answered the call to arms during both World Wars. The field officers of the Survey were converted to commissioned status by virtue of a law that allowed them to be transferred directly into the branches of the armed services, and more than half of them were so transferred during both conflicts. The civilian weather observers, laborers, meteorologists, cartographers, scientists and administrators of both the Weather Bureau (later Service) and C&GS also signed up in droves; more than 1,100 personnel of the C&GS and 700 from the Weather Service voluntarily joined the fighting forces during World War II. Both organizations contributed greatly to final victory – the C&GS through its maps, charts, field survey, and intelligence-gathering, and the Weather Service through world-wide weather forecasts, climate studies, and special weather products to help plan the movements of men, ships, and aircraft.

Merchant Marine

The Merchant Marine Act of 1936 provided for establishment of federal training for Merchant Marine officers. The US Merchant Marine Cadet Corps was officially founded on March 15, 1938 under the auspices of the US Maritime Commission, chaired by Joseph P. Kennedy – a position taken over by Admiral Emory Scott Land. Initially, training of cadets was given aboard government-subsidized ships under the direction of shore-based Port Inspector-Instructors. In February 1942 administration of the training program was turned over to the Coast Guard, but in July 1942 it was given to the War Shipping Administration.

US Coast Guard Auxiliary

With the prospect of war approaching, Congress deemed it necessary to augment the US Coast Guard with a civilian reserve force, and on June 23, 1939 the US Coast Guard Reserve was authorized. This organization would be administered by the Commandant of the USCG and composed of unpaid, volunteer US citizens who owned motorboats or yachts. In 1941, Congress created a military Coast Guard reserve, renaming the volunteer Coast Guard Reserve the US Coast Guard Auxiliary. In 1939 Congress defined the Reserve's purpose as being "to assist the Coast Guard: (1) to promote safety and to effect rescues on and over the high seas and on navigable waters; (2) to promote efficiency in the operation of motorboats and yachts; (3) to foster a wider knowledge of, and better compliance with, the laws, rules, and regulations governing the operation of motorboats and yachts; (4) to facilitate other operations of the Coast Guard."

On November 1, 1941 President Roosevelt signed an order transferring the Coast Guard from the Treasury Department to the Navy Department. A few weeks later the Japanese attacked Pearl Harbor, and the Coast Guard's reserve system was put to the ultimate test. On the night of December 7, amid rumors of Japanese invasion, 20 Coast Guard Auxiliarists from the 13th District took their boats out of Seattle on the service's first wartime patrol cruise. In May 1942 the Secretary of the Navy authorized uniforms for the Coast Guard Auxiliary.

To help counter the imagined threat of enemy saboteurs, in the light of a lack of sufficient coastal patrols, the USCG established a program similar to the Local Defence Volunteers (later, Home Guard) in Britain, whereby qualified volunteer individuals or entire units would be assigned as Temporary members of the US Coast Guard Reserve (TRs). To make this program more effective many Auxiliarists were commissioned as temporary officers of the Coast Guard Reserve. Each Temporary member of the Reserve, even though on non-paid duty status with the Coast Guard, was a member of the armed forces of the United States. All were required to swear allegiance to the US and all were subject to military discipline and punishment under what is now called the Uniform Code of Military Justice (UCMJ). Arming of the Temporary reserves and their boats rested with the local Coast Guard officer in charge. The Coast Guard Auxiliary was a non-military, non-armed service; when Auxiliarists were on duty as Temporary Reserves, they were no longer Auxiliarists but military personnel – but as soon as they went off duty, they returned to Auxiliary status.

The **Beach Patrol** program began on October 12, 1942; the Coast Guard's job was to patrol, and alert the Army of any possible dangers. Both horse and dog patrols were established, as were a network of watchtowers. In addition, the 45 bridges spanning the Inland Waterway from St Augustine to Key West were guarded. The Coast Guard checked both land and sea traffic. By spring 1943, there were 2,000 men along with 200 dogs and 500 horses on duty in the 7th Naval District. The mounted patrol covered 20 miles of beach per night, the foot patrol 12 miles.

Perhaps the Auxiliary's most important contribution to the war effort was the **Volunteer Port Security Force**. An executive order of February 1942 directed the Secretary of the Navy to take the necessary steps to prevent "sabotage and subversive activities" on the nation's waterfronts. The task of protecting the countless warehouses, piers and other facilities that kept the American shipping industry in business fell to the Coast Guard, which in turn delegated it to the Reserve and the Auxiliary. Every port city within the United States had a Coast Guard officer with the title of Captain of the Port, who was placed in charge of a Port Security Force consisting of TRs, Auxiliarists, and other civilians recruited for the purpose; the precise organizational structure varied from city to city. The Coast Guard set up a Reserve Training School in Philadelphia to train TRs in such subjects as anti-espionage methods, fire prevention, customs inspections and small-arms handling. Eventually some 20,000 Reservists and Auxiliarists participated in port security patrols. About 2,000 women also enrolled as "TR SPARs," attending to the mountainous paperwork that despatched ships, cargoes and troops overseas.

As the war went on and the Coast Guard's resources were stretched thinner, Auxiliarists and TRs were called upon to fill gaps wherever active duty Coast Guardsmen left them. Auxiliarists' boats patrolled the waterfronts and inlets looking for saboteurs, enemy agents and fires. At least one unit of Temporary Reservists, recruited from the Auxiliary, patrolled east coast beaches on horseback. Other Auxiliarists manned lookout and lifesaving stations near their homes, freeing regular Coast Guardsmen for sea duty. When a flood struck St Louis in the spring of 1943, Coast Guard Auxiliarists and Reservists evacuated 7,000 people and thousands of head of livestock. By the end of the war the Coast Guard Auxiliary boasted a total membership of 67,533, of which 53,214 men and women were serving as Temporary members of the Reserve. At the end of the war the Coast Guard TRs were "honorably disenrolled," but many remained Auxiliarists for years afterward. Wartime service had earned them no veterans' benefits and precious little other public recognition. In 1946 the TRs were awarded the Victory Medal; Auxiliarists who had not joined the Reserve had to be satisfied with the thanks of Adm Waesche: "The Auxiliary during the war years was indispensable. Many thousands of you served faithfully and loyally as Auxiliarists and as temporary members of the CG Reserve, performing hundreds of tasks and relieving thousands of Coast Guardsmen for duty outside the continental limits. The Coast Guard is deeply appreciative of this service."

AERONAUTICAL SERVICES

Air Transport Command

On May 29, 1941 the Air Corps created the Ferrying Command to fly aircraft from US factories to Canada and to Atlantic ports for delivery to Great Britain. By the coming of war in December that year the Command had delivered approximately 1,350 planes for Britain, and had also established an air transport service between Washington and Britain. On July 1, 1941 LtCol Caleb V. Haynes made the first flight in a modified B-24 Liberator bomber by way of Newfoundland, and soon the Command was making regular flights to England. With Maj Curtis E. LeMay as co-pilot, Haynes began a pioneering 26,000-mile survey trip on August 31, 1941, from the US to the Middle East and back, via Brazil and the southern Atlantic. That year a start was also made on building airbases along a southern flight corridor from the US to Australia, and regular service along this route began in 1942.

When the US went to war the War Department was forced to turn to the civil airlines for aid in securing additional aircraft, developing new flight routes, and transporting cargo and passengers on contract over domestic and foreign routes. Thousands of new transport planes were ordered, reservist pilots were called to active duty, and hundreds of civilians were commissioned as officers and made "service pilots" – a rating for which physical qualifications were lower than for a combat pilot. On June 20, 1942 the Ferrying Command became the Air Transport Command (ATC), with world-wide responsibility for ferrying aircraft, for transporting personnel, materiel, and mail, and for maintaining air route facilities outside the US. By the end of 1944, ATC had more than 3,000 transport aircraft in use and had become the

"lifeline" of the Army Air Forces, flying to every part of the world where US troops served. When the war ended the ATC was the largest airline in the world. Most of the civilians returned to their respective airlines and air transport services. The ATC became the Military Air Transport Command after the creation of the US Air Force in 1947 (from 1965, the Military Airlift Command).

British Flying Training Schools

To this day, a bit of Britain can be found in a small Florida town: 23 Royal Air Force Cadets sleep eternally in a peaceful cemetery in Arcadia. They came across the Atlantic to learn how to fly, as thousands of others went elsewhere in the USA and to Commonwealth countries which shared America's advantages as a flight school: predictably good weather for many months of the year, and lack of interference from enemy intruders. The British Isles were crowded with operational airfields from which the RAF was waging war against Germany; flying training schools required space, and safety from enemy raids. Royal Air Force training airfields were bombed for the first time on August 13, 1940; and eight months later, on April 13, 1941, it was agreed at a conference between RAF Air Vice-Marshal Garrod and USAAF General H.H. Arnold that a part of the training facilities in the United States would be turned over to the British. Arrangements for the establishment of six British flying training schools in the US had already been made, and these now took shape, several months before Pearl Harbor. Southern Florida received its share, and the city of Arcadia in south-central Florida became a pivotal point for two important British training schools: the British No.5 at Riddle Field, Clewiston, which opened in September 1941, and the US School at Carlstrom and Dorr Fields, Arcadia – Carlstrom, a World War I Army airfield, reopened in June 1941. From 1941 to 1945 the Lodwick School of Aeronautics of Lakeland trained 8,825 cadets, of which 1,327 were British, while the schools in Arcadia and Clewiston trained well over 1,879 British cadets. Of the six British flying training schools in the United States, BFTS No.5 at Clewiston received the highest performance rating.

Civil Air Patrol

The CAP was conceived in the late 1930s by legendary New Jersey aviation advocate Gill Robb Wilson, who foresaw aviation's role in war and general aviation's potential to supplement America's military operations. With the help of New York Mayor Fiorello La Guardia, the new Civil Air Patrol was established on December 1, 1941, just days before Pearl Harbor, and initially came under the Office of Civil Defense. During the war CAP members flew antisabotage, antisubmarine and border patrols, target towing and search-and-rescue missions, and also aided in recruiting Army Air Force trainees. The CAP consisted of more than 75,000 volunteers on April 29, 1943 when it was transferred to the War Department as an auxiliary of the AAF.

Members of the Civil Air Patrol pose as if at a briefing; note the distinctive red epaulets and the shoulder patches on their khaki shirts. Just visible on the left chest of the man second from right is the early-style CAP pilot's wings badge.

The CAP insignia – a red three-blade propeller in the Civil Defense white-triangle-in-blue-circle – began to appear on civilian aircraft everywhere. Although originally envisaged as limited to liaison and reconnaissance flights, the CAP mission expanded when German U-boats began to attack US shipping off the east coast of the United States. On antisubmarine patrol, CAP crews in light planes ranged as far as 150 miles out to sea. During 18 months of antisubmarine patrols in 1942–43, CAP crews flew 244,600 hours, the equivalent of 24 million miles. They reported 173 enemy subs and summoned aid for 91 ships in distress and for 363 survivors of submarine attacks. After some CAP planes began carrying bombs and depth charges, they attacked 57 subs, allegedly sinking or damaging at least two; others were destroyed by AAF or Navy planes and ships called out by CAP pilots by radio. During these antisubmarine patrol operations alone, the CAP lost 90 airplanes and 26 members. In all the CAP flew half a million hours during the war, and 64 aviators lost their lives.

Relief Wings Inc

This organization, sponsored by leaders in aviation, medical, civic, church and business life, was formed in May 1940; it was projected as a permanent non-profit humanitarian air service, to provide air ambulances and disaster relief by air to civilians, in time of peace or war, at home or abroad. During World War II the registered facilities of Relief Wings were available for immediate emergency service. There were 11 sectional units with jurisdiction over 38 states. By 1943 some 200 flight surgeons and flight nurses had enrolled, and were available to other agencies such as the Civil Air Patrol, the American Red Cross and the Office of Civil Defense.

Female flight nurses of Relief Wings wore a horizon-blue suit with a tailored white shirt. The belted jacket had a pleated work-back, and a skirt described as concealing the trouser or culotte feature designed for climbing in and out of planes. The overseas cap was worn with Relief Wings pin and the particular Corps emblem. The organization's wings were designed to show the various offices and qualifications of the wearer, such as: National Coordination Chairman, Sectional Director, State Leader of Volunteer Flight Surgeons, Corps Leader of Volunteer Flight Nurses, Flight Leader of Aircraft, Aircraft Owner or Pilot Volunteer, and Amateur Radio Operator.

Excellent portrait photo of a CAP pilot, displaying the Antisubmarine Patrol patch on his left forearm – see also Plate E3. He also wears the later version of the pilot's wings; this replaced the earlier form, which were felt to be rather too "Third Reich" in outline.

Women's Auxiliary Ferrying Squadron & Women's Airforce Service Pilots

The WAFS came into existence on September 5, 1942 at Newcastle Army Air Base, Delaware, and Nancy Love was appointed its director. The WAFS were qualified female pilots hired by the War Department and working under the supervision of the Ferrying Division of the Air Transport Command. Their duties were to ferry light liasion and training planes within the continental limits of the United States, thereby relieving male pilots for combat duty or for ferrying planes to combat zones. Some of the basic requirements to serve with the WAFS were: American citizenship, age between 21 and 35, high school education, Commercial Pilot's Certificate, 500 hours of flight time with 50 hours within the past year, 200 horse-power rating, and two letters of recommendation. The average pay rate at the time was $250 a month with $6 per diem while on ferrying missions. Initially the WAFS uniform consisted of a jacket, skirt, and slacks of light gray gabardine. The single-breasted jacket had four patch pockets with buttoned flaps, a belt of self material, and epaulets. Civilian pilot wings were worn above the left pocket, and on the left shoulder an Army Air Force emblem above a tab bearing the letters "W.A.F.S." in blue on light gray. Within a month of the establishment of the WAFS another organization, the Women's Flying Training Detachment (WFTD), was formed in order to train pilots for later service in the WAFS.

Various leather flight jackets are worn by these female ferry pilots photographed in front of a B-17 Flying Fortress; the "Fifinella" emblem of the WASPs painted on some of them dates the picture to 1943 at the earliest. (National Archives)

In 1943 the Women's Airforce Service Pilots (WASP – an acronym penned by Gen "Hap" Arnold) became the official name of all women's auxiliary flight organizations. On August 5, 1943 the WAFS and WFTD were absorbed into the WASP. Jacqueline Cochran became the organization's new Director of Women Pilots, and Nancy Love was appointed as a WASP executive in the Ferrying Division of the Air Transport Command. By the time that the WASP was disbanded in December 1944 the women pilots had flown 12,650 planes over a collective distance of 9,224,000 miles within its short 27-month history. Of the 916 WASPs, only 38 were lost in flight accidents.

Despite the creation of the WASP in August 1943 and the merging of the WAFS and WFTD, it was not until July 1, 1944 that 1,600 blouses were ordered from the Philadelphia Quartmaster Depot. The first graduates of the newly formed WASP receiving the new uniforms first, and it was the end of summer 1944 before it was standardized for the existing members. The walking-out uniform consisted of a Santiago-blue blouse with three wooden buttons, a matching skirt, and a white shirt with a black necktie. A unique feature of the uniform was the beret headgear, with a gilt American eagle for pilots or the winged propeller for trainees (though the latter was never actually worn). In addition, a Santiago-blue battledress blouse similiar in style to the US Army's "Ike" jacket, and matching trousers also proved popular, and WASP pilots wore them on ferrying missions. Amongst flight gear, the A-2 and B-3 leather flight jackets were the most commonly issued models worn by these women pilots.

BELOW LEFT **The Army maintained a close relationship with the Civilian Conservation Corps, as evidenced by the uniform worn here at some date before 1939. This young worker displays the CCC Honor Award for distinguished service.**

BELOW RIGHT **By 1939 a new spruce-green CCC uniform had been introduced; it was issued through the Army's Philadelphia Quartermaster Depot.**

THE WORKFORCE

The Civilian Conservation Corps

At the height of the Depression, President Roosevelt had called the 73rd Congress into emergency session on March 9, 1933 to authorize his proposal to recruit thousands of unemployed young men, enroll them in a peacetime army, and send them into battle against the destruction and erosion of America's natural resources. Before it was over, more than 3 million men had engaged in a massive salvage operation – the most popular experiment of the New Deal, and the beginning of the Civilian Conservation Corps (CCC). Regular and reserve Army officers, and regulars of the Navy, Marine Corps and Coast Guard were temporarily assigned to command camps and companies; the Army also provided logistical support such as transportation, clothing, food, and medical care. The departments of Agriculture and Interior were responsible for planning and organizing work to be performed in every state, while the Department of Labor, through its state and local relief offices, was responsible for the selection and enrollment of applicants. All four agencies performed minor miracles in coordination with a National Director, Robert Fechner, a union vice-president personally picked by FDR. The administrative Advisory Council, composed of representatives of the secretaries of War, Labor, Agriculture and Interior, would serve for the duration. Controversial, but important to the President's hopes for the program, was the appointment of an educational adviser to every camp; eventually more than 40,000 illiterates were taught to read and write and others acquired further skills.

In April 1937 a further Act of Congress formally created a Civilian Conservation Corps, but FDR's attempt to put it on a permanent footing failed. Nevertheless, just some of the CCC's accomplishments during its existence included: 3,470 fire towers erected; 97,000 miles of fire roads built; 4,235,000 man-days devoted to fighting fires, and more than 3 billion trees planted. Five hundred camps were under the control of the Soil Conservation Service, eventually arresting erosion on more than 20 million acres. The CCC also made outstanding contributions in the development of national, state, county, and metropolitan parks. From 83 camps in 15 western states another 7,153,000 man-days were expended on such programs as protecting range for the Grazing Service and natural wildlife habitats, stream improvement, restocking of fish, and building dams for water conservation.

A popular, if idealized image of a Woman Ordnance Worker. Note the distinctive headscarf, with the repeated motif of a flaming ordnance bomb – see Plate H1.

51

Military representatives and factory officials display an Army-Navy "E" pennant for excellence, as awarded to some plants to recognize outstanding achievements in wartime production.

By late summer 1941 a lack of applicants, desertions, and the number of enrollees leaving for conventional jobs had reduced the Corps from some 300,000 to fewer than 200,000 men in about 900 camps. There were also signs that public opinion was beginning to question the need for it now that unemployment had practically disappeared; and after Pearl Harbor any federal project not directly associated with the war effort was under threat. A joint committee of Congress recommended that the CCC be abolished by July 1, 1942, and despite a last-ditch attempt to vote its continued funding it survived for only a matter of months.

"Rosie the Riveter:" Women Ordnance Workers

"Daddy, what did you do in the war?" was a popular question for war veterans, but World War II provided a whole new twist – "Mommy, what did *you* do in the war?" Rose Will Monroe probably best represented the new way of life whereby the women who raised the post-World War II baby boom generation had already provided much of the labor for producing the materiel of war. Monroe (who died on May 31, 1997 in Clarksdale, Indiana) became famous as "Rosie the Riveter," Norman Rockwell depicted her for the *Saturday Evening Post*, and she became well known as a War Bond promoter, as well as a poster-girl flexing her muscles while wearing a Women Ordnance Worker bandanna. But Rosie was not just another pin-up; she was the real thing. She was working as a riveter building B-29 and B-24 bombers at the Willow Run Aircraft Factory in Ypsilanti, Michigan, when she was discovered by actor Walter Pidgeon. Because she fitted the image of the Kay Kyser hit song, "Rosie the Riveter," she was selected to appear in a short film that promoted War Bonds throughout the nation's theaters.

After Pearl Harbor the young men of America poured out of the factories and offices to line up at the recruiting offices, and the young women of America lined up at the factories and arsenals to fill the traditional male jobs left vacant by those who went off to fight. Those who were involved in the production of military hardware became known as Women Ordnance Workers (WOWs). These women wore hardhats and coveralls, and pulled the same load as many of the men they replaced; they operated heavy cranes, milling machines, and countless other heavy tools that most women had never heard of before the war. The WOWs also made weapons, bagged gunpowder, crated ammunition and did whatever else was asked of them so that their fathers, husbands, sons, and sweethearts could win the war and come back home again.

The "Rosie the Riveter" movement is credited with helping push the number of working women to 20 million during the four years of war – a 57 percent jump from 1940. About 300,000 women were employed in War Department activities in November 1943. The WOW bandanna became a well-known symbol of the 85,000 women who worked directly for the Ordnance Department. An advertisement in the July–August 1943 issue of *Army Ordnance* enthused: "… and she wears the WOW bandanna. Water Repellent. Washable. Dust Proof. The 'WOW' Bandanna, designed in accordance with US Army specification, is an attractive, safe, and unifying head covering to identify Women Ordnance Workers. About 27in square, it is available either in Ordnance red with white Ordnance insignia, or in white with red Ordnance insignia. Every woman in your plant will want one – it's a 'WOW' for morale! $3.75 per dozen, net FOB, New York. Manufactured under authorization from the Army Ordnance Department. We invite your inquiry. Brian Fabrics Corporation, 1441 Broadway, New York City."

These women helped their workplaces, both civilian and government, to be recognized by the military. Army/Navy "E" Award pennants for Excellence in Production were given to businesses that supported the war effort; the award ceremony was elaborate, with senior military officers present and Airforce fly-overs provided. Some of the WOWs formed a uniformed organization referred to as the Women Ordnance Workers Incorporated. It was first organized at the Hurley Machine Company in Chicago on September 22, 1942 and was in no way connected with the Ordnance Department or the government. Members wore a trim air force-blue uniform with patch pockets, brown leather

WOWs gather in front of a Treasury flag, awarded to companies in which 90 percent of employees invested regularly in War Bonds. Note that some of these women wear caps or coveralls with ordnance workers' badges.

The role of women in World War II naturally did not end with temporarily replacing the men in civilian jobs. In 1942 Congress established the Women's Army Auxiliary Corps (WAAC), and several hundred thousand women volunteered to "free a man to fight." Although issued military-style uniforms, and replacing soldiers in clerical and other non-combat related jobs, the WAACs had no official military status until 1943, when they officially became part of the armed forces as the Women's Army Corps (WAC). See Men-at-Arms 357, *World War II Allied Women's Services.*

A Women's Land Army volunteer wearing the distinctive WLA armband with her work clothes.

belt, open-neck white blouse or gilet and an overseas cap. WOWS Inc had as its symbol a shield superimposed upon crossed cannons, bearing the letters "WOW," and topped by eagle wings and the monogram "USA."

Women's Land Army

The WLA had its origins in World War I, when it was created in response to President Woodrow Wilson's call for an increase in food production; the organization worked in cooperation with the United States Food Administration. The "farmerettes" relieved the shortage of men who had gone off to fight, and tended the crops in farmlands across the country. The same call went out in World War II; the Women's Land Army was part of the Registration of Farm Labor program organized and developed through the state offices of the United States Employment Service that was a part of the War Manpower Commission. The Department of Agriculture had outlined to Congress five necessary steps to meet the farm labor shortage: (1) Keep on the farms as many experienced managers as possible; (2) recruit more industrial labor from the cities; (3) use the services of more women and young people, training the inexperienced; (4) develop efficient ways of transporting migrant farm workers to areas where they are needed; (5) take good farmers off poor land and put them on good land.

A statistical estimate made by the War Manpower Commission figured that 70 percent more women were working on the farms in the summer of 1942 than in the summer of 1940. The WLA had a force of 50,000 women who worked on farms and ranches across the United States. By the end of the war it was a familiar sight to see women driving trucks and tractors along American highways. The standard "uniform" of the WLA consisted of blue denim overalls, a long-sleeve shirt, and a unique WLA hat that almost resembled the bonnets worn in the pioneering days of the Old West.

CHILDREN AT WAR

Boy and Girl Scouts

The Boy Scouts of America (BSA) was inspired by and modeled on the Boy Scout Association, established by Baden-Powell in Britain in 1908; it was incorporated on February 8, 1910. Girl Scouting in the United States began on March 12, 1912 when founder Juliette "Daisy" Gordon Low organized the first Girl Scout troop meeting with 18 girls in Savannah, Georgia. During both World Wars, Scouts helped out on the home front by selling defense bonds, growing victory gardens, and collecting waste fat and scrap iron. Girl Scouts became famous for selling their Girl Scout Cookies as their annual fundraiser, which they began in 1917 – a tradition that has long outlasted the World Wars.

The BSA implemented the Sea Scouts program in 1912 – basically a nautical/naval equivalent for older youths. In 1917 Scouter James "Kimo" Wilder came on board as Chief Seascout; his revamping of the program in an attempt to invigorate the movement was unsuccessful, and he stepped aside in 1923 for Cmdr Thomas J. Keane. Keane's reorganized Sea Scout program was basically that which still exists today; he developed the naval-style uniforms, office titles and insignia, four-level advancement program of Apprentice, Ordinary, Able, and Quartermaster, and other features. In 1935, Sea Scouts became part of the larger Senior Scout Division of the BSA. In addition, the Girl Scouts also launched the Mariner Girl Scout program in October 1934, for older Girl Scouts interested in outdoor water-based activities. By the end of that year 12 Mariner ships were registered, and the first two handbooks – *Launching a Girl Scout Mariner Ship,* and *Charting the Course of a Girl Scout Mariner Ship* – were published.

With a membership of more than 27,000 boys, Sea Scouting served the United States well in World War II, when Keane was recalled to active service in the Navy and resigned his position as national director. Thousands of former and active Sea Scouts joined the Navy, and they made a tremendous impression on Adm Chester Nimitz, who sincerely believed that Sea Scouts were better trained and better equipped to face the enemy and the elements. (In 1949 Sea Scouts were renamed Sea Explorers, as part of the renaming of Senior Scouts to Explorers. The Mariner Girl Scout program remains active but in a smaller form; most girls have instead joined the Sea Scouts, which has been co-ed since 1971.)

The Scouts contributed in other areas of war work. Their part in training State Guards in fieldcraft at the Tactical School has already been mentioned (see under "State Defense Forces" above). In mid-1942 an order by the President made the Scouts official government dispatch-bearers for the Office of War Information; since there were 1,589,281 of them, this must have been the largest messenger service in the world. Eventually the Scouts service was reduced by some half-million who, leaving the Office of War Information, joined the Civil Defense services, but 424,000 still remained to carry the OWI's voluminous dispatches. War Savings became of major importance, and before VJ-Day the Scouts had succeeded in selling an impressive $1,800 millon-worth. By then their collection of paper, though it had been slowed down by the War Production Board, had reached the figure of 240,019 tons – an amount sufficient to make, among other things, 3.5 million protective

A popular fashion for children was miniature copies of armed forces uniforms; this proud youngster sports a copy of the Army Air Corps uniform.

The Boy Scouts of America was the largest of the children's organizations; it contributed considerably to the war effort, volunteering for everything from scrap collection drives and War Bond sales to performing government messenger service and instructing State Guards in fieldcraft. (National Archives)

bands for 1,000lb bombs, more than 5 million similar bands for 500lb bombs, packing for more than 16 million 75mm shells, some 64 million containers for blood plasma, and 93.59 million cartons each containing ten cartridges for inflating life-floats.

By 1945 more than 67,000 Scouts were working in victory gardens, and more than 20,000 possessed gardens over 400 feet square; these were eligible for "Green Thumb" certificates and MacArthur medals. They also helped the Forestry Service by planting 142,103 trees. Blood banks were established all over the country which received blood donations from Scouts, who also worked in large numbers with the hospitals. They provided entertainments for the Armed Forces, collecting more than 3 million musical instruments, gramophone records and furniture for Services hospitals. As elsewhere, the number of former Scouts and Scoutmasters who won distinction in battle when serving with the Armed Forces was very large. Nearly 2 million Scouts had served by the time the war was won, and the Scouts of America then concentrated on raising the World Friendship Fund launched by their National Council, with the object of helping the reorganization of Scouting in Allied countries devastated by the war.

Victory Corps

As Americans became more involved in the wartime volunteer organizations, on September 25, 1942 Commissioner of Education John W. Studebaker established the Victory Corps, upon the recommendation of his advisory Wartime Commission, to increase the involvement of high school students. The purpose of this organization was to prepare high school students to aid in the war effort both on the home front and the frontlines. Both girls and boys from white and African American schools participated. In order to be a member a student needed to participate in a physical fitness program, enroll in a war-effort class, and volunteer for at least one extracurricular wartime activity. The physical fitness programs were essential, because military officials were alarmed by the poor condition of recent enlistees.

At the advent of the war high school curricula in Maryland had been altered to accommodate war-effort classes; by modification of industrial arts and vocational-industrial classes, students could learn about machinery, the fundamentals of electricity, radios, the canning of food, aeronautics, first aid, rifle shooting, and other pertinent topics. Due to its proximity to Washington, DC, Maryland had the first three Victory Corps programs: Ellicott City High School in Howard County, and Sherwood High School and Montgomery Blair Senior High School, both in Montgomery County. As the war progressed 126 of the 145 Maryland county high schools and all of Baltimore City's high schools established Victory Corps. As the hostilities approached a close the Victory Corps program was phased out, beginning in June 1944.

Uniforms of any type or style differed from school to school, but the Victory Corps did use a series of standardized insignia. Many students wore an oddly shaped light gray overseas-style cap which had the top corners squared off. A red "V" patch was sewn to the front left side of the cap. A round blue patch could be sewn over the top of the "V" for students involved with the following activities: Agriculture (wheat within cogwheel), Aviation (three-blade propeller), Community Service (Geneva cross), Land (American eagle), and Sea (fouled anchor).

SELECT BIBLIOGRAPHY

Bailey, Ronald H., *The Home Front: USA* (Alexandria, VA; Time-Life Books, 1977)

Billinger, Robert D., *Hitler's Soldiers in the Sunshine State* (Gainesville, FL; University Press of Florida, 2000)

Brayley, Martin J., *The British Home Front, 1939–45* (Elite 109; Osprey Publishing, 2005)

Brayley, Martin J., *World War II Allied Nursing Services* (Men-at-Arms 370; Osprey Publishing, 2002)

Breuer, William B., *The Air Raid Warden was a Spy and Other Tales from Home-Front America in World War II* (Edison, NJ; Castle Books, 2003)

Burnett, Betty, *St Louis at War: The Story of a City, 1941–1945* (St Louis, MO; The Patrice Press, 1987)

Burnham, Frank A., *Aerial Search: The CAP Story* (Fallbrook, CA; Aero Publishers Inc, 1974)

Coffey, Frank, *50 Years of the USO* (New York; Brassey's (US) Inc, 1991)

Cohen, Stan, *The Tree Army: A Pictorial History of the Civilian Conservation Corps, 1933–1942* (Missoula, MT; Pictorial Histories Publishing Company Inc, 1980)

Cohen, Stan, & Don DeNevi, *They Came to Destroy America: The FBI Goes to War Against Nazi Spies & Saboteurs...* (Missoula, MT; Pictorial Histories Publishing Company Inc, 2003)

Cole, David J., PhD, *Florida World War II Heritage Trail* (Tallahassee, FL; Florida Department of State, 2004)

de Quesada, Alejandro M., "Guarding the Skies Over Pass-A-Grille", *Veterans Sentinel* Volume 1, Number 6 (February 1994)

de Quesada, Alejandro M., "Pass-A-Grille Steeled for War", *Yesterday in Florida*, Number 20, Winter 2005

de Quesada, Alejandro M., "Soldiers of the Reich in Tampa Bay", *Pastimes*, Volume 2, Number 1 (Fall 1995)

de Quesada, Alejandro M., "Some Corner of an American Field", *The Armourer*, Issue 12 (Nov–Dec 1995)

de Quesada, Alejandro M., *The Royal Air Force Over Florida* (Charleston, SC; Arcadia Publishing, 1998) de Quesada, Alejandro M., *World War Two in Tampa Bay* (Charleston, SC; Arcadia Publishing, 1997)

Dies, Martin, *The Trojan Horse in America: A Report to the Nation* (New York; Dodd, Mead & Company, 1940)

Duke, David, & Iris, *State Guard Distinctive Insignia* (Shawnee, KS; K & M Collectibles Inc, 2004)

Emert, Phyllis Raybin (ed), *World War II: On the Homefront* (Carlisle, MA; Discovery Enterprises Ltd, 1995)

Freitus, Joseph & Anne, *Florida: The War Years 1938–1945* (Niceville, FL; Wind Canyon Publishing Inc, 1998)

Jacobs, Martin, *World War II Homefront Collectibles* (Iola, WS; Krause Publications, 2000)

Johnson, Stephen D., & Gary S. Poppleton, *Cloth Insignia of the US State Guards and State Defense Forces* (Hendersonville, TN; Richard Smith Military Books, 1993)

Jones, Wilbur D., & Carroll Robbins, *Hawaii Goes to War: The Aftermath of Pearl Harbor* (Shippensburg, PA; White Mane Books, 2001)

Keefer, Louis E., *From Maine to Mexico with America's Private Pilots in the Fight Against Nazi U-Boats* (Reston, VA; COTU Publishing, 1997)

Krammer, Arnold, *Nazi Prisoners of War in America* (New York: Stein and Day, 1979)

Mormino, Gary R., *Hillsborough County Goes to War: The Home-Front, 1940–1950* (Tampa, FL; USF Libraries, 2001)

Petersen, George, *American Women at War in World War II Vol. I* (Springfield, VA; NCHS Inc, no date – r/p of wartime uniform references of various women's organizations)

Rexford, Oscar Whitelaw, *Battlestars & Doughnuts: World War II Clubmobile Experiences of Mary Metcalfe Rexford* (St Louis, MO; The Patrice Press, 1989)

Ross, Mary Steele, *American Women in Uniform: Complete descriptions, duties, qualifications, and requirements of 27 Women's Organizations* (Garden City, NY; Garden City Publishing Co Inc, 1943)

Sage-Gagne, Waneta, *Pilots in the Sun: Primary Pilot Training Schools in Lakeland and Avon Park, Florida 1940–1945* (Lakeland, FL: Friends of the Library, 1990)

Smith, Jill Holcomb, *Dressed for Duty: America's Women in Uniform 1898–1973* (San Jose, CA: R. James Bender Publishing; *Vol 1,* 2001; *Vol 2,* 2004)

Tilley, John A., *The United States Coast Guard Auxiliary: A History 1939–1999* (Washington, DC; United States Coast Guard, 2002)

Weatherford, Doris, *American Women and World War Two* (New York: Facts on File Inc, 1990)

Wynne, Lewis N. (ed), *Florida at War* (Dade City, FL; Saint Leo College, 1993)

PLATE COMMENTARIES

A: AMERICAN FASCISTS: The German-American *Bund*, Camp Nordland, 1939–42
A1: Fritz Kuhn, *Bundesführer*
A2: Drum Major, *Jugendschaft, Ortsgruppe Brooklyn*
A3: Youth Leader, *Frauenschaft*

Fritz Kuhn's uniform (**A1**) consisted of a light gray, single-breasted coat with black cap, epaulets, cuffs and upper part of the open collar, and silver piping and buttons. He wore this over a gray poplin shirt with turndown collar, two breast pockets and shoulder straps, with a black four-in-hand tie and the *Bund* badge. For duty indoors he wore long black trousers without cuffs, black shoes and socks. The *Ordnungsdienst* left armband has a black ground with a white stripe near the top and bottom edges, and the black and gold insignia of the *Bund* centered between a gold "O" and "D." The Drum Major (**A2**) of the *Jugendschaft* is wearing *Hitler Jugend* (Hitler Youth) articles imported from Germany: the "swallow's-nest" shoulder ornaments with white fringes, black leather belt with HJ steel buckle, and HJ knife. The female youth leader (**A3**) is wearing a uniform similiar in style to those worn by the German *Bund Deutsche Mädel* (BDM) and *NS-Frauenschaft* girls' and women's organizations. She is holding a white oak pole with the rigid white triangular

Members of the Citizens Defense Corps serving as medical volunteers; see also Plate B1. (Pinellas County Historical Commission)

pennant bearing a black *siegrune* within a red circle. (Inset) The *Bund* stickpin badge.

B: CIVIL DEFENSE, 1941–45
B1: US Citizen's Defense Corps
B2: Blackout Warden
B3: Spotter, Aircraft Warning Service
B4: Educational advisor, Civilian Conservation Corps

The Citizen's Defense Corps woman (**B1**) wears a suit in slate-blue rayon with a matching overseas cap, a white cotton shirt and navy-blue tie. The embroidered insignia for the staff was a blue circle and white triangle, with "CD" superimposed in red; it is attached to the left sleeve one inch below the shoulder seam. On her collars are a pair of emblems consisting of the blue circle and white triangle, with a star over "CDC" in red superimposed, all superimposed over "US" in silver. On the left side of her cap is a small "CD" patch; note also the purse in uniform color. The warden (**B2**) is wearing a high-domed, white-painted helmet with gray canvas chinstraps, and the CD emblem on the front; a World War I-style trench coat; and an armband with a blue circle and white triangle, the superimposed red and white stripes identifying his role as an air raid warden. He is equipped with a whistle, a black plastic trench flashlight clipped to the cloth belt of his coat, and a slung gas mask. The female Aircraft Warning Service observer (**B3**) is identified only by a blue armband with a yellow-winged white disc and the words "U.S. ARMY/AIR FORCE/AWS/OBSERVER." The CCC education officer (**B4**) is wearing an Army-style uniform consisting of a spruce-green gabardine jacket with green buttons and olive-green sleeve braids, with three small buttons on each cuff. On the left sleeve near the shoulder is the CCC patch. On the right collar is a diamond-shaped gilt insignia with the letters "CCC," and on the left collar a burning lamp emblem. Rank insignia consisting of two small embroidered discs of gold bullion are worn on the outside center of the coat sleeves, one inch above the braid. The Army-style cap has a gilt emblem of an American eagle below the letters "CCC."

C: MARITIME ORGANIZATIONS, 1941–45
C1: Third Class Petty Officer, United States Coast Guard Auxiliary
C2: Chief Petty Officer, United States Maritime Service
C3: Ship's Master, Army Transportation Service
C4: Coxswain, Sea Scouts, BSA

Nearly all the maritime services wore uniforms identical in style and cut; usually the only differences were that service's distinctive insignia and rank structure. The Coast Guard Auxiliarist (**C1**) is wearing an officer-style single-breasted jacket that had been adopted by the auxiliaries and temporary reservists performing shore duties. On his collar are two brass USCG Auxiliary emblems. On his right wrist he has a silver chained bracelet consisting of a World War II USN-style dogtag (oval disc) – this was the service award given to auxiliarists during the war for devoting more than 600 hours' service. The Maritime Service

Members of the US Public Health Service attached to a service branch wore the uniform of that assignment; here two such employees compare Navy and Army uniforms with USPHS insignia – see also Plate D4.

(Merchant Marine) CPO **(C2)** wears a dark blue uniform with a USMS rating patch on his right sleeve, and on his left an armband for Maritime Shore Patrol. His white pistol belt supports a black leather holster for his .38in revolver. The ATS officer **(C3)** wears the dark blue double-breasted coat with six buttons, and on each sleeve four gold stripes in full lace beneath a gold upright fouled anchor. The Scout **(C4)** is wearing a US Navy jumper, trousers and white "dixie cup" cap, the latter with the Sea Scout emblem in silver – the BSA eagle superimposed on an anchor – pinned to the front. The following insignia are worn on the jumper: at the top of the right sleeve, a round light blue patch with the American shield in red, white and blue, bordered in yellow; midway between shoulder and elbow is the coxswain's insignia; and just above the cuff is the bugler's device, embroidered in white with red tassels. On his left sleeve he has a white-bordered, white-lettered shoulder tab "JERSEY SHORE"; about an inch and a half below this are white block numerals "49"; 2in below this is a red-bordered patch with a white sailing ship on dark blue waters beneath light blue sky. On his right breast is the title

"SEA SCOUTS B.S.A." in white embroidery. **(Inset)** The Walt Disney-designed insignia of the "Corsair Fleet," volunteer CG Auxiliarists who performed antisubmarine patrols on the East Coast in their own small craft.

D: HUMANITARIAN ORGANIZATIONS, 1941–45
D1: Clubmobile Volunteer, American Red Cross
D2: First lieutenant, American Women's Hospital Reserve Corps
D3: Cadet Nurse, United States Public Health Service
D4: Senior Surgeon, United States Public Health Service
The Red Cross clubmobile volunteer **(D1)** has a gray-blue rayon jacket in British battledress style, with women's slacks tucked into knitted socks with brown leather ankle boots. On her left shoulder is a Red Cross patch lettered with "*AMERICAN RED CROSS*/MILITARY WELFARE SERVICE." Her cap is of the same material, and has a red enameled Geneva cross emblem on the front. She is showing off her OD field jacket, with many souvenir military unit patches given to her by grateful soldiers. The AWHRC officer **(D2)** is wearing a grayish-tan military-cut uniform consisting of a six-gore skirt with one pleat in front, and button fastening; a tan military cut shirt with long sleeves, maroon shoulder straps, one-button cuffs, and a maroon rayon tie; a fitted blouse with hip and breast pockets, shoulder straps, half-inch silk braid bands around the sleeves 3in above the ends, joined "RC" devices

ABOVE LEFT **Female member of the Civil Air Patrol posing with the "Wolf Squadron" badge of the Corpus Christi, Texas, Coastal Patrol Base. (National Archives)**

ABOVE RIGHT **Willa Beatrice Brown, the first African American woman to be commissioned in the CAP; she went on to be a flight instructor. Here she wears a male-style coat buttoning from left to right. Note cap badge; red epaulets; lapel badges – "C.A.P." above Army Air Force-style winged propellers; and the earlier, Germanic-looking pilot's wings. (NARA, courtesy Alex Bielakowski)**

on the collar points and caduceus emblems on the lapels. Her rank is designated by a pair of bronze metal discs worn on the shoulder straps, over the crossed stitching at the end and parallel with the seam. Above her left pocket are three ribbons: the Award of Merit, Efficiency Award, and Distinguished Service Award. The Cadet Nurse Corps uniform (**D3**) consists of a cadet-gray wool coat and skirt; the USPHS Cadet Nurse patch is worn on the left sleeve, and a pair of silver USPHS emblems on the lapels. A cadet-gray wool beret-style headgear with the USPHS emblem in silver completes the uniform. The senior surgeon (**D4**) is wearing an Army-style officers' uniform with gilt USPHS emblems for medical officers on his collars and Army officer's cap.

E: AERONAUTICAL ORGANIZATIONS, 1941–45
E1: Flight instructor, British Flight Training School No.5
E2: First Officer/Station Manager, Air Transport Command
E3: Major, 3rd Coastal Patrol, Civil Air Patrol
E4: Pilot, Women's Airforce Service Pilots

The flight instructor (**E1**) of BFTS No.5 at Clewiston is wearing a Royal Air Force-style cap emblem and pilot's wings on his shirt, but with the king's crown above the wreathed eagle replaced with "BFTS". The ATC first officer (**E2**) is wearing an Army-style officer's uniform with ATC co-pilot wings, and on the ends of his shoulder straps are his ATC distinctive rank discs. On his left sleeve is a large blue patch with a white triangle and "US" in blue superimposed, designating him as a non-combatant. His rank is further identified by two bars at the end of the shoulder straps of the trenchcoat. The CAP major (**E3**) wears Army-style khaki cap, shirt, and pants. On the lower left sleeve is his antisubmarine patrol insignia, consisting of a bomb dropping onto a submarine, in gold stitching on a gold-bordered black background. He is holding his brown leather A-2 flight jacket, with the painted squadron insignia of the 3rd Coastal Patrol. The female pilot (**E4**) is wearing her old WAFS uniform while awaiting issue of the new WASP uniform during summer 1944. Her A-2 jacket shows her organization's new emblem, "Fifinella" – a gremlin designed by Disney Studios.

When the WAFS and WFTD were amalgamated into the WASP in 1943, a new uniform of so-called Santiago blue was designed and issued. Note the distinctive beret headgear. As well as this four-pocket coat there was a matching waist-length "Ike" jacket that proved popular for flying duties.

F: STATE DEFENSE FORCES, 1941–45
F1: Sergeant, Florida Defense Force
F2: Captain, 4th Regiment, Missouri State Guard
F3: Private, Women's Ambulance and Defense Corps of America
Typical of most state guard units, the Florida Defense Force **(F1)** wore Army-style khaki overseas caps (without piping), shirt and pants. On the left shoulder is an orange twill disc with a light gray embroidered border and title "FLORIDA DEFENSE FORCE." On the left side of the overseas cap is a small orange twill disc with a green alligator and the letters "FDF" in white **(inset)**. In 1943 the Florida Defense Force changed its name to Florida State Guard. The Missouri State Guard captain **(F2)** is wearing an Army-style olive drab gabardine coat and pants, khaki

shirt and tie; on the left sleeve is the patch for the 4th Regiment. Instead of the US Army officer's cap emblem bearing the Great Seal of the United States, his displays the Missouri state seal. The WADCA member of the "Santa Monica Defense Force" **(F3)** is wearing an Army-style khaki overseas cap, shirt and long skirt (a four-pocket khaki blouse was also worn). A WADCA patch was worn on the left sleeve of the shirt and blouse, as well as on the overseas cap. In addition, in most cases an arched tab bearing the wearer's home town or unit designation was worn below the organization's patch on the sleeve; **(inset)** is that of the Santa Barbara (Hollywood) unit. She is armed with an M1917 bolt-action rifle.

G: PATRIOTIC ORGANIZATIONS, 1941–45
G1: Second lieutenant, Motor Transport, American Women's Volunteer Services
G2. National Commander, Daughters of the Defenders of the Republic
G3. Entertainer, United Services Organization
G4. Volunteer, Junior Commandos
The AWVS Motor Transport uniform **(G1)** consisted of a four-pocket suit in gray-blue wool with four large brass buttons, topped with a matching cap with the round MTS emblem in front, and completed by a white cotton shirt and navy-blue tie; the AWVS patch is worn on the left shoulder. The Daughters of the Defenders of the Republic **(G2)** wore a uniform in Army khaki wool, the tunic having epaulets, these four pockets, and a brown leather belt. The skirt was a wrap-around style, worn over trousers that come down over the knees, and was designed so that the skirt itself could be removed and used as a blanket to cover patients during first aid treatments. The khaki visored hat was in "Pershing" style, bearing the emblem of the DDR. As commanding officer this woman wears a gold braid on the shoulder straps, an aqua-blue cloth collar and a hat band edged with gold braid; her rank is further identified by three gold sleeve rings on blue cuffs, and three gold bars across the right lapel. The USO entertainer **(G3)** is wearing an Army-style officer's uniform but cut for a woman, with the "USO CAMP SHOWS" patch worn on the left side of the overseas cap as well as on her jacket. The youthful member of the Junior Commandos **(G4)** is wearing an Army-style khaki shirt with a black necktie tucked in. An improvised arm band displays a black hand-stenciled emblem consisting of "JC" over three stars within an oval; it is fashioned out of cardboard covered with white cloth, with two straps for fastening. On his shirt he is wearing a Theodore Roosevelt Medal for academic achievement with a red, white and blue ribbon. He is seen bringing a World War I helmet to the scrap drive – probably without his father's knowledge…

H: THE WORK FORCE, 1941–45
H1: Woman Ordnance Worker, Springfield Armory
H2: Auxiliary Military Police, St Louis Ordnance Plant
H3: Volunteer, Women's Land Army
The oil-stained blue coveralls and heavy brown work boots are typical of clothing worn by both men and women industrial workers; **(H1)** is also wearing the red head scarf with white flaming bomb designs that became the symbol

ABOVE **Unit photo of members of the 3rd Bn, 28th Infantry Regt, Massachusetts State Guard, taken at Camp O'Connor, Framlingham, in July 1945. All except the cook wear khakis, with rank on collar or sleeves and an MSG left shoulder patch. See also Plate F.**

RIGHT **Barbara Ohman, photographed in 2005 wearing her old WLA sunbonnet-style hat – see Plate H – at an event commemorating the 60th anniversary of the end of World War II. (Author's photo)**

of the Women Ordnance Workers. The auxiliary military police officer **(H2)** is wearing a blue police-type uniform loosely based on the military model; on the left pocket is a factory picture ID, and on the left sleeve is a large shield patch lettered "AUXILIARY MILITARY POLICE." The cap is of the police type, with paneled sides; and he is wearing a black Sam Browne-type belt with an open holster for a .38in Colt revolver, a common sidearm among American policemen. He is raising the Army/Navy "E" Award pennant that has been awarded to his ordnance plant for excellent performance. The Women's Land Army Volunteer **(H3)** is wearing the WLA's unique sun bonnet-type headgear with the organization's emblem on the crown, repeating that on her armband.

INDEX

Figures in **bold** refer to illustrations.